JavaScript Fetch API for Complete Beginners

By Laurence Lars Svekis

For more content and to learn more, visit
https://basescripts.com/

Source Code https://github.com/lsvekis/-
JavaScript-Fetch-API-for-Complete-Beginners/

Book Introduction

Welcome to **"JavaScript Fetch API for Complete Beginners"**, a resource designed to help you unlock the potential of working with APIs in modern web development. APIs (Application Programming Interfaces) have become the backbone of the interconnected world we live in, enabling seamless data exchange between applications. This book is your gateway to mastering the Fetch API, a modern and powerful JavaScript interface that simplifies the process of making HTTP requests.

Whether you're a beginner looking to learn the fundamentals or an intermediate developer aiming to solidify your understanding of API interactions, this book provides a structured approach to learning through detailed explanations, real-world examples, and hands-on exercises.

Who is This Book For?

This book is designed for:

- **Beginners**: Those new to JavaScript and eager to understand how to fetch and work with data from APIs.
- **Web Developers**: Professionals or students looking to deepen their understanding of client-server communication.
- **Self-Learners**: Individuals who enjoy step-by-step tutorials and practical examples to enhance their coding skills.
- **Instructors**: Educators seeking a clear and concise resource to teach the fundamentals of the Fetch API.

No prior experience with APIs is required, though a basic understanding of JavaScript will be helpful.

What Will You Learn?

By the end of this book, you will:

1. Understand the fundamentals of APIs and their importance in modern web development.
2. Master the Fetch API to make GET, POST, PUT, DELETE, and PATCH requests.
3. Learn how to handle responses, parse JSON data, and deal with errors effectively.
4. Gain insights into advanced concepts like query parameters, authentication, and working with RESTful APIs.
5. Build real-world applications using hands-on exercises and projects that reinforce your knowledge.

How to Use the Book

This book is organized to maximize your learning:

- **Step-by-Step Progression**: Start with the basics and progressively move to more advanced topics.
- **Hands-On Exercises**: Each chapter includes practical exercises to apply what you've learned.
- **Multiple-Choice Quizzes**: Test your understanding of key concepts at the end of chapters.
- **Example Projects**: Build mini-projects that simulate real-world API interactions.
- **Code Samples**: Explore downloadable code examples on GitHub to follow along and experiment.

Take your time with each section and don't hesitate to revisit topics or examples to solidify your understanding.

Why This Book Works

This book is crafted with a learner-focused approach:

- **Clear Explanations**: Concepts are broken down into simple terms, ensuring clarity.
- **Practical Applications**: Learn through doing, with examples grounded in real-world scenarios.
- **Structured Learning Path**: A logical progression of topics ensures you build on your knowledge incrementally.
- **Interactive Learning**: Exercises, quizzes, and projects keep you engaged and help reinforce your understanding.
- **Community Insights**: Draws from the experiences of educators and developers to address common challenges and questions.

APIs are integral to the functionality of modern applications, and mastering the Fetch API is a pivotal skill for any aspiring or experienced web developer. This book equips you with the tools and knowledge to confidently work with APIs, empowering you to build interactive, data-driven applications.

As you turn the final page of this book, you'll not only have a solid foundation in the Fetch API but also the confidence to tackle more advanced API-related challenges. Remember, learning doesn't stop here — explore, experiment, and continue building on your newfound skills.

Introduction to APIs

Definition: What is an API?

An **Application Programming Interface (API)** is a set of rules, routines, and protocols that allows software applications to communicate with each other. Think of an API like a menu in a restaurant. When you visit a restaurant, you look at the menu to see what dishes you can order. Once you place an order, the kitchen (the "backend") prepares the dish and sends it to you. Similarly, an API provides an interface that tells developers (the customers) how to request data or services from a server (the kitchen), and then it returns a structured response.

Explanation of Application Programming Interfaces

- **Bridge Between Software**: APIs act as a contract or middle layer, defining how data is requested and delivered without revealing the complexity of how the service actually works internally.
- **Consistency**: By following a set of predefined endpoints and data formats, different teams can work on independent parts of a project without breaking each other's code.
- **Reusability**: Once an API is built, other applications can reuse the same interface to interact with the underlying data or functionality.

Real-World Examples of APIs

- **Food Delivery Apps**: The application on your phone interacts with a backend server that checks which restaurants are available, the estimated delivery time, and your order status. The phone app sends requests and receives structured responses—most often in JSON format.

- **Social Media**: When other websites let you "Sign in with Facebook" or "Share via Twitter," they use Facebook's or Twitter's APIs to verify users and share data.
- **Weather Apps**: Most weather apps don't host weather data themselves; they connect to an external weather service's API to fetch forecasts and current conditions.

Types of APIs

Although there are many protocols and architectural styles for APIs, three common ones are:

1. **REST APIs (Representational State Transfer)**
   - **Popularity**: Widely used due to their simplicity and scalability.
   - **HTTP Methods**: Typically use familiar methods like GET, POST, PUT, and DELETE.
   - **Stateless Architecture**: Each request from the client to the server must contain all the information needed to understand and process the request.
2. **SOAP (Simple Object Access Protocol)**
   - **XML-Based**: Heavily reliant on XML for request and response formatting.
   - **More Rigid**: Often includes more formal contracts and stricter standards. Historically popular in enterprise environments.
3. **GraphQL**
   - **Query Language**: Allows clients to request exactly the data they need and no more.
   - **Single Endpoint**: Uses a single URL for most interactions, with queries specifying the desired data structure.

Importance of APIs in Modern Development

1. **Connecting Frontend and Backend**: APIs separate the user interface (e.g., a React or Vue web app) from the data layer (e.g., a Node.js or Python server), making it easier to maintain and update each side independently.
2. **Data Retrieval and Interaction with External Services**: Many applications rely on external APIs for features like payment processing, map data, or user authentication. Instead of building everything in-house, developers can plug into existing services.
3. **Scalability and Extensibility**: With a well-designed API, businesses can expand capabilities by integrating new features or services without rewriting entire systems.

Coding Example: A Simple "Hello World" RESTful Endpoint

While we'll dive deeper into coding examples later, here's a quick look at how a **very simple** RESTful API endpoint might be set up using Node.js and Express. This example shows the essence of an API: you send a request to a specific URL, and you get a structured response.

```
// hello-api.js
const express = require('express');
const app = express();
const PORT = 3000;

// Define a simple GET endpoint
app.get('/hello', (req, res) => {
  res.json({ message: 'Hello, World!' });
});
```

```
app.listen(PORT, () => {
  console.log(`Server is running on
http://localhost:${PORT}`);
});
```

1. **Endpoint**: `/hello`
2. **HTTP Method**: GET
3. **Response Format**: JSON containing `{ message: 'Hello, World!' }`

From a client perspective (like a web browser or another application), making a GET request to `http://localhost:3000/hello` returns the JSON response.

Exercises

1. **Concept Clarification**
    - In your own words, explain what an API is and why it's useful in software development.
    - Briefly describe how APIs contribute to modern web applications.
2. **Identify the Components**
    - In the "Hello World" endpoint above, which part is the "frontend," and which is the "backend"?
    - How would you test this endpoint once the server is running?
3. **Research Task**

- Pick one popular online service (e.g., Twitter, Spotify, or Google Maps). Find out if they provide a public API. Write a short summary of what that API can do.

4. **Brainstorming**
   - List three different types of data or functionality you might want to access via an API (e.g., movie information, book information, music recommendations).
   - For each type, think of an existing service that might offer such an API.

Multiple Choice Quiz

1. **What does the term "API" stand for?**
   A. Applied Protocol Integration
   B. Application Programming Interface
   C. Authorized Public Interface
   D. Abstract Processing Implementation

2. **Which of the following is NOT a characteristic of RESTful APIs?**
   A. They often use JSON for request and response formats
   B. They require a WSDL (Web Services Description Language) file
   C. They use HTTP methods like GET, POST, PUT, and DELETE
   D. They are typically stateless

3. **Which statement best describes the role of APIs in modern applications?**

   A. APIs are only used for internal communication and cannot be exposed publicly.

   B. APIs make it more difficult for applications to share data with each other.

   C. APIs act as a contract between different software components, simplifying communication and data exchange.

   D. APIs are only used when a database is not available.

4. **Which of the following is a key benefit of using APIs?**

   A. They eliminate the need for any security considerations.

   B. They only work with JSON data.

   C. They allow you to integrate existing services instead of building all features from scratch.

   D. They guarantee your application will never have any bugs.

5. **Which of these API types is known for its flexible query language where the client controls the exact data returned?**

   A. SOAP

   B. REST

   C. GraphQL

   D. OData

Detailed Answers to the Quiz

1. **(B) Application Programming Interface**
   - This is the correct expansion of "API." An API defines how software components should interact.

2. **(B) They require a WSDL (Web Services Description Language) file**

13

- WSDL is associated with SOAP APIs, not RESTful APIs. REST doesn't rely on WSDL; it often uses simple documentation or formats like OpenAPI/Swagger instead.

3. **(C) APIs act as a contract between different software components, simplifying communication and data exchange**
   - This answer describes precisely how APIs allow different parts of a system (or different systems entirely) to communicate in a structured way.

4. **(C) They allow you to integrate existing services instead of building all features from scratch**
   - One major benefit of APIs is that developers can reuse services (like payment gateways, social networks, or analytics) without needing to reinvent the wheel.

5. **(C) GraphQL**
   - GraphQL is a query language for APIs that allows clients to request exactly the data they need. It differs from REST and SOAP in this respect.

Wrap-Up

At this stage, you should have a clear understanding of what APIs are, why they're vital in modern software development, and the different styles in which they can be implemented. The next steps will dive deeper into **REST APIs** and how to utilize them using **JavaScript's Fetch API**, focusing on practical coding exercises and real-world applications.

Introduction to the Fetch API

The Fetch API is a modern, built-in JavaScript interface that allows you to make HTTP requests to servers directly from the browser. It was introduced to simplify the process of retrieving data and interacting with APIs compared to older techniques like `XMLHttpRequest`. With the Fetch API, you can request and send data asynchronously—making it a cornerstone of modern web development.

What is the Fetch API?

- **Native JavaScript API**: Provided by browsers without the need for external libraries.
- **Promise-Based**: Returns a Promise, making asynchronous code easier to handle compared to callbacks.
- **Modern Browser Compatibility**: Supported by all modern browsers. (For older browsers, a polyfill can be used.)

Unlike the old `XMLHttpRequest` object, the Fetch API uses promises by default, which offers a cleaner and more intuitive way of working with asynchronous operations.

Key Features

1. **Asynchronous and Non-Blocking**
   - The browser doesn't freeze while the request is in progress.
   - Your code can continue executing other tasks while waiting for the network response.
2. **Promise-Based**
   - Easy error handling using `.then()` and `.catch()`.

o   More readable than nested callbacks.
3. **Stream Handling**
    o   Allows for more advanced use cases, such as working with streams and partial data.
4. **Extensible**
    o   You can customize requests with headers, body content, authentication tokens, and more.

Basic Syntax

The Fetch API's basic usage typically involves calling `fetch()` with a URL and then chaining `.then()` for success and `.catch()` for errors:

```
fetch('https://some-api.com/data')
  .then(response => {
    // The "response" represents the HTTP
response.
    // Before accessing the actual data, we
often need to parse it (e.g., as JSON).
    return response.json();
  })
  .then(data => {
    // "data" now contains the parsed JSON
from the response.
    console.log('Received Data:', data);
  })
  .catch(error => {
    // Handle any network or parsing errors
    console.error('Error:', error);
```

```
});
```

1. `fetch('https://some-api.com/data')` initiates a network request to the given URL.
2. `.then(response => response.json())`: Fetch resolves the Promise to a `response` object. We usually call `response.json()` (another Promise) to parse the JSON data.
3. `.then(data => ...)`: Once parsing is complete, we can work with the actual data.
4. `.catch(error => ...)`: If the request fails due to network issues or the JSON parsing fails, the error is caught here.

Coding Example: Simple GET Request

Below is a common real-world scenario where you fetch a list of posts from a public API (using a placeholder service).

```
// simple-fetch-get.js

fetch('https://jsonplaceholder.typicode.com/p
osts')
  .then(response => {
    // Convert the response to JSON
    return response.json();
  })
  .then(posts => {
    // 'posts' is now an array of objects
```

```
    // Let's log them or do something with
the data
    console.log('Posts:', posts);
  })
  .catch(error => {
    console.error('Error fetching posts:',
error);
  });
```

What to Observe:

1. **Network Call**: The browser sends a GET request to `https://jsonplaceholder.typicode.com/pos ts`.
2. **Response Parsing**: If successful, `.json()` will parse the JSON body.
3. **Data Usage**: The final `.then()` block handles the parsed data.

Exercises

1. **Basic Fetch Request**
   - Write a function `getUsers()` that fetches user data from `https://jsonplaceholder.typicode.co m/users`.
   - Log each user's `name` and `email` to the console.
2. **Handling Errors**

- Modify your `getUsers()` function to simulate an error. For instance, use a wrong endpoint URL like `https://jsonplaceholder.typicode.com/usersXYZ`.
- Observe what happens in the `.catch()` block.

3. **Experiment with Different APIs**
   - Find a free public API that returns JSON data (e.g., a weather API or a random quote API).
   - Use the Fetch API to retrieve data and log it to the console.
   - Identify any additional steps required, such as including headers or query parameters.

4. **Promise Chain Understanding**
   - Create a Promise chain with at least three `.then()` blocks (for example, one to parse JSON, another to filter data, and a final one to log the result).
   - Ensure you handle errors with `.catch()`.

Multiple Choice Quiz

1. **Which statement best describes the Fetch API?**
   A. A module for importing JSON data from local files.
   B. An asynchronous, promise-based native JavaScript interface for making HTTP requests.
   C. A syntax parser for the JSON format.
   D. A Node.js library for creating server-side applications.

2. **Why is the `.json()` method often used in a Fetch response chain?**

   A. It's required to convert text files into CSV.

   B. It's used to parse JSON data from the response body.

   C. It automatically catches any network errors.

   D. It prevents the Fetch API from throwing exceptions.

3. **Which of the following is NOT a key feature of the Fetch API?**

   A. Using promises for asynchronous handling.

   B. Support for streaming data.

   C. Directly returning JSON data without parsing.

   D. Native browser support without extra libraries.

4. **Which code snippet correctly handles a rejected Fetch promise?**

   A.
```
fetch('https://example.com')
.then(response => response.json())
.then(data => console.log(data))
.finally(error => console.error(error));
```
   B.
```
fetch('https://example.com')
.try(response => response.json())
.then(data => console.log(data));
```
   C.
```
fetch('https://example.com')
.catch(error => console.error(error));
```
   D.
```
fetch('https://example.com')
.then(response => response.json())
.then(data => console.log(data))
.catch(error => console.error(error));
```

5. **When does the `.catch()` block execute in a Fetch chain?**

   A. When the HTTP status is 404.

   B. Whenever an error is thrown during the request or response parsing.

   C. Only when the server sends back non-JSON data.

   D. Only when the browser is offline.

Detailed Answers to the Quiz

1. **(B) An asynchronous, promise-based native JavaScript interface for making HTTP requests.**
   - The Fetch API allows you to request resources asynchronously and returns a promise, which makes error handling and result processing more efficient.

2. **(B) It's used to parse JSON data from the response body.**
   - The `.json()` method reads the response body and parses it as JSON, returning a promise that resolves to the parsed object.

3. **(C) Directly returning JSON data without parsing.**
   - The Fetch API does not return JSON data directly. You must call `.json()` on the response object to parse the body.

4. **(D)** `fetch('https://example.com')`
   `.then(response => response.json())`
   `.then(data => console.log(data))`
   `.catch(error => console.error(error));`
   - This is the standard pattern for handling both success (`.then()`) and failure (`.catch()`) when using Fetch.

5. **(B) Whenever an error is thrown during the request or response parsing.**

○ The `.catch()` block will capture network errors (like being offline) or parsing errors (like invalid JSON). However, an HTTP error status (e.g., 404, 500) does not automatically trigger `.catch()`, unless you explicitly throw an error in a preceding `.then()` block after checking `response.ok`.

Summary

In this section, you learned:

- What the Fetch API is and why it's a modern alternative to `XMLHttpRequest`.
- How promises make the Fetch API more readable and easier to work with.
- The fundamental syntax using `.then()` and `.catch()`.

Up next, you'll see how to handle different HTTP request methods (GET, POST, PUT, DELETE) and expand on error handling strategies to build robust client-side applications.

Understanding HTTP Requests

HTTP (Hypertext Transfer Protocol) is the foundation of data communication on the web. Every time you load a webpage, submit a form, or fetch data from a server, you're using HTTP under the hood. In this section, we'll explore what HTTP is, the common request methods you'll use, and how status codes work.

What Is HTTP?

1. **Protocol for Web Communication**
   - HTTP defines how messages are formatted and transmitted between clients (e.g., web browsers or frontend applications) and servers (where resources or data are hosted).
   - It's a request-response protocol: the client sends a request, and the server returns a response.
2. **Stateless Nature**
   - HTTP is "stateless," meaning each request is independent. The server does not automatically remember any previous requests from the same client. (Sessions or tokens can be used to simulate "state.")
3. **Text-Based**
   - HTTP messages (requests and responses) are primarily text-based, consisting of headers and (optionally) a body.

Request Methods

HTTP includes several methods that define the intended action on a resource (e.g., retrieving or modifying data). Although there are more than a dozen methods, beginners commonly work with these:

1. **GET**
   - **Purpose**: Retrieve data from a server.
   - **Body**: Typically no body is sent with a GET request.
   - **Use Case**: Loading a webpage, fetching a user's profile, or getting a list of posts.
2. **POST**
   - **Purpose**: Send data to a server to create or update a resource.

- o **Body**: Often contains JSON or form data.
- o **Use Case**: Submitting a form, creating a new user, or posting a comment.

3. **PUT**
   - o **Purpose**: Replace an existing resource with new data.
   - o **Body**: Typically JSON or similar.
   - o **Use Case**: Updating all fields of an existing record.

4. **DELETE**
   - o **Purpose**: Remove an existing resource on the server.
   - o **Body**: Rarely used, though possible.
   - o **Use Case**: Deleting a user account or removing a post.

5. **PATCH**
   - o **Purpose**: Partially modify an existing resource.
   - o **Body**: Specifies only the changes rather than a full resource replacement.
   - o **Use Case**: Updating a single field of a record.

Focus for Beginners: You'll primarily use **GET** (to retrieve data) and **POST** (to send data). As you gain more experience, you'll incorporate the other methods for full CRUD functionality (Create, Read, Update, Delete).

HTTP Status Codes

When the server responds to an HTTP request, it includes a **status code** in its response to indicate whether the request was successful, redirected, or failed. Here are some of the most common status codes:

1. **200 OK**

- Meaning: The request was successful.
- Example: A GET request to fetch data returns the requested resource.

2. **201 Created**
   - **Meaning**: A resource was successfully created on the server.
   - **Example**: A POST request to create a new user or post.

3. **400 Bad Request**
   - **Meaning**: The request was invalid, possibly due to incorrect syntax or missing parameters.
   - **Example**: A POST request with malformed JSON in the body.

4. **401 Unauthorized**
   - **Meaning**: The request requires user authentication or the provided credentials are invalid.
   - **Example**: Accessing a protected resource without a valid token.

5. **404 Not Found**
   - **Meaning**: The requested resource could not be found on the server.
   - **Example**: A user tries to fetch a resource that doesn't exist.

6. **500 Internal Server Error**
   - **Meaning**: A generic error message indicating that something went wrong on the server.
   - **Example**: A bug or exception in the server's code caused the request to fail.

Coding Examples

Below are some brief coding examples to illustrate how you might send HTTP requests (GET and POST) with the Fetch API and respond to common status codes.

Example 1: GET Request

```
// fetch-get-example.js

fetch('https://jsonplaceholder.typicode.com/posts/1')
  .then(response => {
    if (!response.ok) {
      // Handle non-2xx HTTP status codes
      throw new Error(`Server responded with status: ${response.status}`);
    }
    return response.json(); // Parse the JSON body
  })
  .then(data => {
    console.log('Fetched Post:', data);
  })
  .catch(error => {
    console.error('Error:', error);
  });
```

- **Key Point**: Checking `response.ok` is a common technique to detect HTTP errors (like 404, 500) before parsing the response body.

Example 2: POST Request

```javascript
// fetch-post-example.js

fetch('https://jsonplaceholder.typicode.com/p
osts', {
  method: 'POST',
  headers: {
    'Content-Type': 'application/json'
  },
  body: JSON.stringify({
    title: 'New Post',
    body: 'This is the content of the new
post.',
    userId: 1
  })
})
  .then(response => {
    if (response.status === 201) {
      return response.json();
    } else {
      throw new Error(`Unexpected status
code: ${response.status}`);
    }
  })
  .then(createdPost => {
    console.log('Created Post:',
createdPost);
  })
  .catch(error => {
    console.error('Error creating post:',
error);
```

```
});
```

- **Key Point:**
  - ○ **Request Method**: Set to POST to create a new resource.
  - ○ **Headers**: Specifies the media type (`application/json`).
  - ○ **Body**: Encoded JSON data representing the new resource.

Exercises

1. **Distinguish Request Methods**
   - ○ Write down a scenario (in plain English) for each request method: GET, POST, PUT, DELETE, and PATCH. For example, "PUT: Replace an entire user profile with new data."
2. **Fetch a Non-Existent Resource**
   - ○ Try fetching a resource that doesn't exist (e.g., `https://jsonplaceholder.typicode.com/posts/99999`).
   - ○ Inspect `response.status` and `response.ok`. Log a custom error message for a 404 response.
3. **Handle Different Status Codes**
   - ○ Modify your GET request example to throw different errors based on different status codes (e.g., a custom error message for 400, 401, 404, 500).
   - ○ Log these messages in the console.
4. **POST Request with Validation**

- ○ Use `fetch` to send a POST request with an empty title or body.
- ○ Check if the server responds with a 400 Bad Request. If so, log a user-friendly message.

Multiple Choice Quiz

1. **Which statement best describes the primary role of HTTP?**
   A. To define how data is routed on internal private networks.
   B. To specify how websites are visually styled with CSS.
   C. To establish a request-response protocol for data exchange between clients and servers.
   D. To compile JavaScript on the server.
2. **Which HTTP method is typically used to retrieve data without modifying it?**
   A. GET
   B. POST
   C. PUT
   D. DELETE
3. **Which status code indicates that a resource was successfully created?**
   A. 200
   B. 201
   C. 404
   D. 500

4. You send a request to fetch data from an API endpoint, but the resource doesn't exist. Which status code are you most likely to see?
   A. 200
   B. 401
   C. 403
   D. 404

5. What is the default method used by `fetch()` if none is specified in the options?
   A. GET
   B. POST
   C. PUT
   D. PATCH

Detailed Answers to the Quiz

1. **(C) To establish a request-response protocol for data exchange between clients and servers.**
   - HTTP is the backbone of the web, enabling browsers (clients) to communicate with web servers through standardized requests and responses.

2. **(A) GET**
   - GET is used for fetching or retrieving resources. It should not cause any side effects on the server (i.e., it's considered "safe").

3. **(B) 201**
   - "Created" is specifically used to indicate that a resource has been successfully created on the server.

4. **(D) 404**
   - 404 indicates that the requested resource could not be found on the server.

5. **(A) GET**

   ○ By default, `fetch()` makes a GET request if you do not specify the `method` in the options.

Summary

You now have an overview of how HTTP works, the most common HTTP methods, and the significance of status codes in server responses. Understanding these fundamentals will help you confidently craft and troubleshoot API requests as you continue learning how to use the Fetch API and build RESTful applications.

Making a Simple GET Request

In this chapter, you'll learn how to retrieve data from a public API using the Fetch API. We'll look at how to structure a basic **GET** request, handle promises with `.then()` and `.catch()`, and parse the response data using `.json()`.

Basic Example: Fetching Data from a Public API

Let's use the Dog API as a simple example. This API returns random dog images and breed information in JSON format. Here's how you might fetch a random dog image:

```
// fetch-random-dog.js

fetch('https://dog.ceo/api/breeds/image/rando
m')
```

```javascript
.then(response => {
    // Here, response is an HTTP response
object
    // containing headers, status, etc.
    return response.json();
})
.then(data => {
    // 'data' is now the JavaScript object
parsed from the JSON response
    console.log('Random Dog Image URL:',
data.message);
})
.catch(error => {
    // If a network error occurs or something
goes wrong in the .then() chain,
    // this block will handle it
    console.error('Error fetching data:',
error);
});
```

Key points:

1. **API Endpoint**:
   `https://dog.ceo/api/breeds/image/random`
   returns a JSON object with a `message` property that
   contains the image URL.
2. `.then(response => response.json())`:
   Converts the raw response into a JSON object.
3. `.then(data => {...})`: Gives you access to the
   parsed data so you can use it in your application.

4. `.catch(error => {...})`: Catches network or parsing errors, allowing you to handle them gracefully.

Handling Promises: `.then()` and `.catch()`

A **promise** in JavaScript is an object that represents the eventual completion (or failure) of an asynchronous operation. When you make a network request with `fetch()`, it returns a promise, which can be in one of three states:

1. **Pending**: The request is still ongoing.
2. **Fulfilled**: The request completed successfully, and `.then()` will be called.
3. **Rejected**: The request failed, and `.catch()` will handle the error.

Flow:

1. `fetch(url)` returns a promise that resolves to a **response** object.
2. `response.json()` is also a promise that resolves to the parsed JSON.
3. If any step fails (e.g., the server is down or the response can't be parsed), the `.catch()` block runs.

Parsing JSON: Using `.json()` to Work with API Responses

Most modern APIs return data in JSON format because it's both human-readable and easy for machines to parse. However, the **Fetch API** does not automatically parse JSON for you. You must call `.json()` on the response object:

```
fetch('https://api.example.com/data')
  .then(response => {
    // Even if the server returns valid JSON,
    // you must explicitly parse it with
response.json()
    return response.json();
  })
  .then(parsedData => {
    // Work with your parsed data (which is
now a JavaScript object or array)
    console.log('Parsed Data:', parsedData);
  })
  .catch(error => {
    console.error('Error:', error);
  });
```

Common Patterns for Handling JSON

- **Check for `response.ok`**: It's often wise to check `response.ok` (a boolean) or `response.status` (the numeric status code) before parsing, in case the server returned an error.
- **Handle Large Data**: If the JSON is large, it can take some time to parse. Consider adding UI feedback (e.g., a loading spinner).

Exercises

1. **Practice Fetching a Random Dog Image**

- Write a function `fetchRandomDogImage()` that fetches a random dog image and logs the image URL to the console.
- Add a second `.then()` to log a success message like, "Fetched a random dog image successfully!"

2. **API Documentation Check**
   - Visit another public API (e.g., JSONPlaceholder) and identify an endpoint you'd like to fetch.
   - Make a GET request to retrieve the data. Log a specific field of the response (e.g., a user's name or a post's title).

3. **Error Simulation**
   - Deliberately introduce an error (like changing the URL to a non-existent endpoint).
   - Observe what's logged in the `.catch()` block.
   - Modify your code to display a custom error message if `response.ok` is false.

4. **Chain Multiple `.then()` Blocks**
   - Fetch user data from a public endpoint.
   - In the first `.then()`, parse the JSON.
   - In the second `.then()`, filter or transform the data.
   - Log the final result in a third `.then()`.
   - Make sure you have a `.catch()` at the end to handle any errors.

Multiple Choice Quiz

1. **Which of the following is true about the Fetch API's `.then()` method?**
   A. It is only called if the HTTP status code is 200.
   B. It processes the resolved value of a promise.
   C. It replaces the need for an HTTP status code.
   D. It parses JSON automatically.
2. **What is the main purpose of calling `.json()` on a Fetch response?**
   A. To handle network errors.
   B. To convert the response to a string.
   C. To parse the body of the response as JSON and convert it into a JavaScript object.
   D. To generate an HTML document from the API data.
3. **If you want to log a custom error message when a Fetch request fails, where should you place your code?**
   A. Inside a `.then()` block.
   B. Directly after the `fetch()` call.
   C. Inside a `.catch()` block.
   D. Fetch never fails, so this is unnecessary.
4. **Which of the following best describes a promise?**
   A. It's a synchronous mechanism for handling data.
   B. It's a placeholder object that represents the eventual completion or failure of an asynchronous operation.
   C. It's an array of completed network requests.
   D. It's a structure that guarantees the server will always respond with valid JSON.

5. **Which API might return a random dog image when you call it?**

   A.
   `https://jsonplaceholder.typicode.com/users/1`

   B. `https://dog.ceo/api/breeds/image/random`

   C. `https://catfact.ninja/fact`

   D.
   `https://api.openweathermap.org/data/2.5/weather`

Detailed Answers to the Quiz

1. **(B) It processes the resolved value of a promise.**
   - The `.then()` method is invoked when the promise is fulfilled, passing the resolved value (in this case, an HTTP response).

2. **(C) To parse the body of the response as JSON and convert it into a JavaScript object.**
   - `.json()` transforms the raw data into a JavaScript object, making it easier to work with.

3. **(C) Inside a `.catch()` block.**
   - `.catch()` is specifically designed to handle errors, whether they are network errors or thrown intentionally in the `.then()` chain.

4. **(B) It's a placeholder object that represents the eventual completion or failure of an asynchronous operation.**
   - A promise is an asynchronous concept in JavaScript that resolves or rejects at some point in time.

5. **(B)**
   `https://dog.ceo/api/breeds/image/random`

- ○ This endpoint provides a random dog image in JSON format.

Conclusion

Making a simple GET request in JavaScript using the Fetch API is straightforward once you understand promises and JSON parsing. You've now practiced fetching data from a public API, handling the async flow with `.then()` and `.catch()`, and properly parsing JSON. In the coming chapters, we'll explore more advanced techniques, including different request methods, error handling strategies, and integrating fetched data into your own applications.

Making a POST Request

When working with APIs, **POST** requests allow you to send data to a server to create or update resources. This is different from **GET** requests, which only retrieve data. In this section, you'll learn how to use the Fetch API to send data via POST, specify the correct headers, and parse the server's response.

Sending Data to an API: How POST Differs from GET

1. **Request Method**
   - ○ **GET**: Retrieves existing data from a server (read-only operation).
   - ○ **POST**: Submits new data (or updates) to the server. Often used for creating records in a database or posting form data.
2. **Request Body**

- o **GET** requests typically don't include a request body (they can include query parameters in the URL).
- o **POST** requests usually include a **body** containing the data you want to send in a specific format (e.g., JSON).

3. **Side Effects**
   - o **GET** is considered a "safe" method since it doesn't modify server data.
   - o **POST** can create, update, or modify data on the server side.

Using Fetch for POST

When making a POST request with **fetch()**, you'll include additional configuration options in the second parameter:

```
fetch('https://example.com/api/endpoint', {
  method: 'POST',                // Tells the
server we're sending data
  headers: {
    'Content-Type': 'application/json'  //
Informs the server we're sending JSON
  },
  body: JSON.stringify({         // The request
body, which must be a string
    name: 'John Doe',
    age: 30
  })
})
  .then(response => {
```

```
    // Handle the response from the server
    return response.json();    // Parse the
JSON response
  })
  .then(data => {
    // 'data' is the server's response object
    console.log('Server Response:', data);
  })
  .catch(error => {
    // Catch any network errors or thrown
errors
    console.error('Error:', error);
  });
```

Key Points

- **method**: Set to `'POST'` to indicate data submission.
- **headers**:
    - `'Content-Type'`: `'application/json'`
      tells the server we're sending JSON-formatted data.
- **body**:
    - Must be a string—use `JSON.stringify()` to
      convert a JavaScript object into a JSON string.

Practical Example: Sending a Simple JSON Object to a Test API

A popular test API for demonstrating POST requests is
JSONPlaceholder. You can "create" a post or user, and it will return
a fake response simulating a server action. Although it won't
persist your data, it's perfect for practice.

```
// post-to-jsonplaceholder.js

fetch('https://jsonplaceholder.typicode.com/p
osts', {
  method: 'POST',
  headers: {
    'Content-Type': 'application/json'
  },
  body: JSON.stringify({
    title: 'My New Post',
    body: 'Hello, world!',
    userId: 123
  })
})
  .then(response => response.json())
  .then(createdPost => {
    console.log('Created Post:',
createdPost);
    // Expected response includes an "id"
property (e.g., id: 101)
  })
  .catch(error => {
    console.error('Error creating post:',
error);
  });
```

In this example:

1. **Endpoint:**
   `https://jsonplaceholder.typicode.com/pos`
   `ts` (simulated resource creation).
2. **Request Body**: Contains a `title`, `body`, and `userId`.
3. **Server Response**: Includes an auto-generated `id`, confirming the new resource was "created."

Exercises

1. **Basic POST**
   - Write a function `createUser()` that sends a POST request to `https://jsonplaceholder.typicode.co` `m/users` with a JSON body containing a `name` and an `email`.
   - Log the returned JSON response to the console.
2. **Debugging Errors**
   - Change the endpoint from `https://jsonplaceholder.typicode.co` `m/posts` to something invalid (e.g., `https://jsonplaceholder.typicode.co` `m/postsXYZ`).
   - Observe what happens in the `.catch()` block.
   - Update your code to log a custom error message explaining the failure.
3. **Experiment with Different Content-Types**
   - Although JSON is most common, try sending data with a different content type like `text/plain` or `application/x-www-form-urlencoded` (you'll need to format the body accordingly).

- Note how the server response changes or if it rejects your request.

4. **Practical Integration**
   - Combine a **GET** and a **POST** request. First, **GET** a list of posts from `https://jsonplaceholder.typicode.com/posts`. Then, **POST** a new post.
   - Log both responses, and note how they differ.

Multiple Choice Quiz

1. **Which HTTP method is used to send new data to the server?**
   A. GET
   B. POST
   C. PUT
   D. DELETE

2. **Why do we often set the header `Content-Type: application/json` when making a POST request?**
   A. Because the server won't accept any other format.
   B. To specify that the request body is in JSON format, allowing the server to parse it correctly.
   C. To ensure the server responds with an HTML document.
   D. To compress the request body.

3. **What is the role of JSON.`stringify()` when making a POST request?**

   A. It converts the server response into a readable string.

   B. It is used to parse JSON data coming from the server.

   C. It transforms a JavaScript object into a JSON string for the request body.

   D. It automatically validates the JSON structure on the server.

4. **Which of the following best describes the difference between GET and POST?**

   A. GET modifies data on the server, while POST only retrieves data.

   B. GET is used to retrieve data, while POST sends data to create or update resources.

   C. GET and POST are identical; they only differ in naming.

   D. GET always requires headers, while POST never requires headers.

5. **What happens if you do NOT call JSON.`stringify()` on a JavaScript object before sending it as the body in a POST request?**

   A. The server automatically converts the object to JSON.

   B. The request will fail immediately.

   C. It will throw an error in the `.then()` block.

   D. The server may receive `[object Object]` (or a similar string), likely causing parsing errors.

Detailed Answers to the Quiz

1. **(B) POST**
   - POST is the correct method for sending new data to the server.

2. **(B) To specify that the request body is in JSON format, allowing the server to parse it correctly.**
   - This header lets the server know it should treat the incoming data as JSON.
3. **(C) It transforms a JavaScript object into a JSON string for the request body.**
   - The server expects the request body in a string format for proper parsing.
4. **(B) GET is used to retrieve data, while POST sends data to create or update resources.**
   - By definition, GET is read-only, and POST modifies or creates server-side data.
5. **(D) The server may receive [object Object] (or a similar string), likely causing parsing errors.**
   - Without JSON.stringify(), the browser will send a default string representation of the object, which most servers cannot parse as valid JSON.

Wrap-Up

You've now learned how to **send data to an API** using fetch() with the **POST** method, including how to structure the request body and specify the appropriate headers. In real-world applications, POST requests are central to creating new records, submitting form data, and performing actions that involve changing server-side data. As you progress, you'll encounter variations of this pattern for updating and partially modifying data with methods like **PUT** and **PATCH**.

Error Handling in Fetch

When you make a request using the Fetch API, multiple things can go wrong. Understanding how to handle these potential issues is crucial for building resilient applications. In this chapter, we'll explore the common types of errors, learn how the `.catch()` method works, and discuss strategies for gracefully handling API errors by examining the response status.

Common Issues

1. **Network Errors**
   - Occur when the client (e.g., the browser) cannot reach the server at all.
   - Causes include a lost internet connection, DNS issues, or the server being unreachable.
   - Typically trigger the `.catch()` block of a Fetch promise.
2. **API Errors (e.g., 404, 500)**
   - Occur when the server is reachable but returns an unsuccessful HTTP status code (4xx or 5xx).
   - Examples:
     - **404 Not Found**: The endpoint or resource doesn't exist.
     - **500 Internal Server Error**: The server encountered an error and couldn't process the request.
   - These do **not** automatically trigger `.catch()`. Instead, the promise still resolves, but `response.ok` will be `false`.

Using `.catch()` for Network Errors

When you use `fetch()`, it returns a promise. If the request fails at the **network level** (e.g., no internet connection), the promise is **rejected**, and the `.catch()` block is called:

```
fetch('https://example-nonexistent-
server.com/data')
  .then(response => response.json())
  .then(data => {
    console.log('Data:', data);
  })
  .catch(error => {
    // This will catch issues like
unreachable server or invalid domain
    console.error('Network Error:', error);
  });
```

What `.catch()` Covers and What It Doesn't

- **Covered by `.catch()`:**
    - Network failure, such as being offline or a DNS error.
    - JSON parse error if `.json()` throws an exception (for malformed JSON).
- **Not Covered by `.catch()`:**
    - API errors that return a valid response but with an error status (e.g., 404, 500).
    - In such cases, you must handle them by checking `response.ok` or `response.status`.

Handling API Errors Gracefully

Checking `response.ok`

The `response.ok` property is a convenient way to detect whether the server returned a successful status code (i.e., 2xx). If `response.ok` is `false`, it indicates an HTTP error (4xx or 5xx):

```
fetch('https://jsonplaceholder.typicode.com/posts/99999') // Likely a 404
  .then(response => {
    if (!response.ok) {
      // The HTTP status code is not in the
200-299 range
      throw new Error(`Server error:
${response.status}`);
    }
    return response.json();
  })
  .then(data => {
    console.log('Data:', data);
  })
  .catch(error => {
    // This catch block will handle both
network errors and the error we just threw
    console.error('Fetch Error:',
error.message);
  });
```

1. **`if (!response.ok)`**: Checks if the status code is **not** in the 200–299 range.
2. **`throw new Error(...)`**: If the status isn't OK, manually throw an error. This error is caught by the `.catch()` block.

3. **`response.json()`**: Parses the JSON body only if `response.ok` is true.

Using `response.status`

If you need more granular handling, you can inspect the specific status code:

```javascript
fetch('https://jsonplaceholder.typicode.com/users/99999') // 404
  .then(response => {
    if (response.status === 404) {
      throw new Error('Resource not found (404)');
    } else if (response.status >= 500) {
      throw new Error('Server error (5xx)');
    } else if (!response.ok) {
      throw new Error(`Unexpected status: ${response.status}`);
    }
    return response.json();
  })
  .then(data => {
    console.log('User data:', data);
  })
  .catch(error => {
    console.error('Fetch Error:', error.message);
  });
```

This approach lets you tailor your error messages or application flow depending on the specific code returned.

___

Coding Example: Combining Network and API Error Handling

```
// fetch-error-handling.js
function fetchData() {

fetch('https://jsonplaceholder.typicode.com/u
sers/99999')
    .then(response => {
      if (!response.ok) {
        // Distinguish between different
error statuses if desired
        if (response.status === 404) {
          throw new Error('User not found
(404)');
        } else {
          throw new Error(`Server returned
status ${response.status}`);
        }
      }
      return response.json();
    })
    .then(data => {
      console.log('User Data:', data);
    })
    .catch(error => {
```

```
    // Catch block for both network errors
and manual throws
    console.error('An error occurred:',
error.message);
  });
}


// Execute the function
fetchData();
```

1. **Check `response.ok`**: If it's false, handle it according to the status code.
2. **Manual `throw`**: Converts the "bad response" scenario into a thrown error, which triggers `.catch()`.
3. **`.catch()`**: Displays a user-friendly message or logs a detailed error.

Exercises

1. **Network Error Simulation**
   - Temporarily disable your internet connection or use a made-up domain (e.g., `https://invalid-url-example.com`) in a `fetch()`.
   - Observe what happens in the `.catch()` block.
   - Write a custom error message for network failures.
2. **API Error Handling**

- Use the
  `https://jsonplaceholder.typicode.co
  m/posts/` endpoint and deliberately request a
  non-existent post (e.g., `/99999`).
- Check if `response.ok` is false and
  `response.status` is 404.
- Throw a custom error when status is 404, and catch
  it in `.catch()`.

3. **Specific Status Codes**
   - Create a function that fetches a resource from any
     public API.
   - If `response.status` is 404, log "Not found."
   - If `response.status` is 500 or above, log "Server
     Error."
   - Otherwise, parse and log the data.

4. **Unified Error Handling**
   - Build a small utility function
     `handleErrors(response)` that checks
     `response.ok`. If not okay, throw an error with
     `response.status`.
   - Use this function in multiple fetch requests to
     maintain consistent error handling across your code.

Multiple Choice Quiz

1. **Which type of error does `.catch()` handle by default when using fetch?**

   A. Any HTTP error with a status code of 4xx or 5xx

   B. Only 404 Not Found errors

   C. Network-level errors such as being offline or unreachable servers

   D. The `.catch()` method does not handle any errors by default

2. **If a request returns a 500 Internal Server Error, which statement is correct regarding Fetch?**

   A. The promise will automatically be rejected and trigger `.catch()`.

   B. The promise will still resolve, but `response.ok` will be false.

   C. The response will be parsed as JSON, and `.catch()` will never run.

   D. The browser will automatically retry the request until it succeeds.

3. **Which property is used to determine if an HTTP response indicates a success (2xx) or an error (4xx/5xx)?**

   A. `response.ok`

   B. `response.body`

   C. `response.type`

   D. `response.message`

4. **In order to handle an HTTP error (like 404) in `.catch()`, what must you do in the `.then()` chain?**

   A. Do nothing—`.catch()` automatically handles 404s.

   B. Throw an error manually if `response.ok` is false.

   C. Use the `finally()` method to capture HTTP errors.

   D. Set a special header in the request options.

5. **Why might you want to check `response.status` in addition to `response.ok`?**

   A. `response.ok` only works in older browsers, while `response.status` is modern.

   B. To distinguish different error codes and provide more specific error messages.

   C. It's required for JSON parsing to work correctly.

   D. To automatically retry on certain status codes.

Detailed Answers to the Quiz

1. **(C) Network-level errors such as being offline or unreachable servers**
   - By default, fetch only rejects the promise for network-level failures or if something goes wrong while trying to parse the response as JSON (like invalid JSON).
   - It does **not** automatically reject on HTTP error status codes.

2. **(B) The promise will still resolve, but `response.ok` will be false.**
   - A 500 status code does not make the Fetch promise reject. Instead, it resolves with `ok : false`, and you must handle it in your `.then()`.

3. **(A) `response.ok`**
   - `response.ok` is a boolean that is `true` for 2xx status codes and `false` for 3xx–5xx codes.

4. **(B) Throw an error manually if `response.ok` is false.**

- HTTP errors do not automatically trigger `.catch()` because Fetch treats them as successful responses. You need to explicitly `throw` an error so the promise is rejected.
5. **(B) To distinguish different error codes and provide more specific error messages.**
   - For instance, you might treat 404 differently from 500, or give the user different prompts.

Summary

In this section, you learned to differentiate **network errors** from **API errors** and how to handle both:

- **Network errors**: Automatically trigger `.catch()`.
- **API errors (4xx, 5xx)**: Do **not** trigger `.catch()` by default. Instead, check `response.ok` or `response.status` and throw an error manually.

Mastering error handling is a vital step in creating robust, user-friendly applications that can gracefully manage unexpected problems. Next, we'll delve into more advanced scenarios, like working with authentication and handling timeouts.

Practical Example: Fetching Data and Displaying It

In this chapter, you'll learn how to display data from an API directly on a webpage. We'll build a simple HTML page, fetch data with JavaScript, and then insert that data into the page dynamically. This approach is fundamental in modern web development—powering dashboards, blogs, and social media feeds.

Scenario: Displaying a List of Items

Imagine you have a task to show a list of users fetched from an external API. For demonstration, we'll use the JSONPlaceholder service, which provides fake data for testing. Specifically, we'll fetch user data and display each user's name, username, and email address.

HTML and JavaScript Integration

Basic HTML Structure

Create a file called **index.html** with the following structure:

```
<!DOCTYPE html>
<html lang="en">
<head>
  <meta charset="UTF-8">
  <title>User List</title>
  <!-- Optional: Link to a CSS file or
include inline styles -->
  <style>
    /* Basic styling for the container and
user list */
    body {
```

```css
  font-family: Arial, sans-serif;
  margin: 20px;
}

h1 {
  text-align: center;
}

#userList {
  display: flex;
  flex-wrap: wrap;
  gap: 20px;
  list-style-type: none;
  padding: 0;
}

.user-item {
  background-color: #f7f7f7;
  border: 1px solid #ccc;
  border-radius: 5px;
  padding: 15px;
  width: 200px;
  box-shadow: 1px 1px 3px rgba(0, 0, 0,
0.1);
  }

.user-item h2 {
  font-size: 1.1rem;
  margin: 0 0 10px;
}
```

```css
    .user-item p {
      margin: 5px 0;
    }
  </style>
</head>
<body>
  <h1>List of Users</h1>
  <!-- An unordered list that will hold our
user items -->
  <ul id="userList"></ul>


  <!-- Include your JavaScript at the end of
the body -->
  <script src="script.js"></script>
</body>
</html>
```

Fetching and Dynamically Rendering the Data

1. **Create `script.js`** in the same folder as `index.html`.
2. **Fetch User Data**: Use `fetch()` to call the API endpoint: `https://jsonplaceholder.typicode.com/users`.
3. **Insert Data into HTML**: Dynamically create `<li>` elements (or any desired HTML structure) to display user information.

`script.js`:

```javascript
document.addEventListener('DOMContentLoaded',
() => {
  const userList =
document.getElementById('userList');
```

```javascript
// Fetch user data from JSONPlaceholder

fetch('https://jsonplaceholder.typicode.com/u
sers')
    .then(response => {
      if (!response.ok) {
        throw new Error(`Error fetching
users: ${response.status}`);
      }
      return response.json();
    })
    .then(users => {
      // For each user, create a list item
and append it to the userList
      users.forEach(user => {
        const listItem =
document.createElement('li');
        listItem.className = 'user-item';

        listItem.innerHTML = `
          <h2>${user.name}</h2>
          <p><strong>Username:</strong>
${user.username}</p>
          <p><strong>Email:</strong>
${user.email}</p>
        `;
        userList.appendChild(listItem);
      });
    })
    .catch(error => {
```

```
      console.error('Failed to fetch user
data:', error.message);
      userList.innerHTML = `<li>Oops!
Something went wrong while fetching
users.</li>`;
    });
});
```

How It Works:

1. **document.addEventListener('DOMContentLoa ded', ...)**: Ensures the HTML is fully loaded before we run our JavaScript.
2. **fetch('https://jsonplaceholder.typicode. com/users')**: Sends a **GET** request to retrieve the user list.
3. **.then(response => response.json())**: Parses the JSON response into a JavaScript array of user objects.
4. **users.forEach(user => {...})**: Iterates over the array, creating new DOM elements for each user.
5. **.catch(error => {...})**: Handles any network or parsing errors.

Styling the Output

In the example above, we added some basic inline CSS. You can further enhance the design by:

- Adding hover effects for each user card.
- Adjusting fonts, colors, and spacing to match your project's design.

- Making the layout responsive for mobile devices.

Exercises

1. **Custom Fields**
   - Modify the user list to also display the user's address (e.g., `user.address.street` and `user.address.city`).
   - Experiment with nested properties in the JSON object to show additional information.
2. **Error Message Customization**
   - Intentionally break the URL (e.g., by adding `/xyz`) to force an error.
   - In the `.catch()` block, display a more user-friendly message in the HTML instead of just logging to the console.
3. **Loading Indicator**
   - Before starting the fetch call, insert a "Loading…" message on the page.
   - Once the fetch is complete (success or fail), remove or replace that message.
4. **Filter Results**
   - Add an `<input>` field and a button. On button click, filter the displayed users by name or username.
   - You'll need to store the fetched data in a variable and re-render the list.
5. **Pagination Practice** (Optional, more advanced)
   - Explore how you might add pagination if the API or data set is large.

○ Simulate it by only showing a subset of users at a time (e.g., 5 per page).

Multiple Choice Quiz

1. **Which element in `index.html` is intended to hold the dynamically created list items?**
   A. `<p id="userList">`
   B. `<ul id="userList">`
   C. `<table id="userList">`
   D. `<div id="userList">`

2. **What does `response.json()` do in the Fetch API?**
   A. Converts JSON data into a JavaScript object or array.
   B. Automatically validates the data structure on the server.
   C. Displays the JSON in the browser console.
   D. It handles all HTTP errors automatically.

3. **In the provided example, where is the `<script>` tag placed and why?**
   A. In the `<head>` to load JavaScript before the page content for faster execution.
   B. At the end of the `<body>` so that the HTML elements are loaded before the JavaScript runs.
   C. Outside of the `<html>` tag so it doesn't interfere with DOM loading.
   D. In the `<title>` tag to keep the page title and script consolidated.

4. **What does `userList.innerHTML` do in the `.catch()` block when an error occurs?**

   A. It appends new content to existing elements in the DOM.

   B. It clears the existing `<ul>` content and replaces it with the specified HTML message.

   C. It hides the `<ul>` element entirely.

   D. It restarts the fetch process automatically.

5. **If you wanted to display additional user details (e.g., phone, website, company), how could you achieve this?**

   A. Add new properties to the `<li>` element's `innerHTML` that reference `user.phone`, `user.website`, etc.

   B. It is not possible because the API only allows name, username, and email.

   C. Change the request from GET to POST.

   D. Create a new HTML element for each user property using an external library only.

Detailed Answers to the Quiz

1. **(B) `<ul id="userList">`**
   - The HTML snippet shows `<ul id="userList">` as the container for our dynamically created list items.

2. **(A) Converts JSON data into a JavaScript object or array.**
   - The `.json()` method reads the raw response body and parses it as JSON, returning the result as a JS object or array.

3. **(B) At the end of the `<body>` so that the HTML elements are loaded before the JavaScript runs.**
   - Placing the script tag at the end ensures the DOM is available before the code tries to manipulate it.

4. **(B) It clears the existing `<ul>` content and replaces it with the specified HTML message.**
   - ○ Using `innerHTML = "<li>...</li>"` removes any current HTML within `<ul>` and inserts the new content.

5. **(A) Add new properties to the `<li>` element's `innerHTML` that reference `user.phone`, `user.website`, etc.**
   - ○ The JSONPlaceholder API provides these additional properties, so you can display them just as you do with `user.name` or `user.email`.

Conclusion

You have now learned how to **integrate Fetch with a basic HTML layout**, retrieve data from an API, and dynamically display it in a browser. This knowledge can be expanded upon to build entire web applications—from simple blogs to complex data dashboards. Next, we'll explore how to handle forms and user input to create truly interactive pages that can both receive and send data via APIs.

Practical Example: Submitting Data with a Form

In this section, you'll learn how to build a web form that collects user input, submits that data to an API using a POST request, and provides feedback based on the success or failure of the operation. This example will walk you through capturing form data in JavaScript, sending it as JSON via a POST request, and displaying a success or error message to the user.

Scenario: User Inputs Data to Add a New Post

Imagine a blog platform where users can create new posts. You need to build a simple form where a user can type in a title and content for the new post. When the user submits the form, the data will be sent via a POST request to an API endpoint that handles posts (for demonstration purposes, we'll use JSONPlaceholder, which simulates resource creation).

HTML Form and JavaScript Integration

Step 1: Create the HTML Form

Create a file named **new-post.html** with the following structure:

```html
<!DOCTYPE html>
<html lang="en">
<head>
  <meta charset="UTF-8">
  <title>Create New Post</title>
  <style>
    body {
      font-family: Arial, sans-serif;
      margin: 20px;
    }
    form {
      max-width: 400px;
      margin: auto;
      border: 1px solid #ccc;
```

```css
  padding: 20px;
  border-radius: 5px;
  background-color: #f9f9f9;
}
label {
  display: block;
  margin-bottom: 8px;
  font-weight: bold;
}
input, textarea {
  width: 100%;
  padding: 8px;
  margin-bottom: 15px;
  border: 1px solid #ddd;
  border-radius: 4px;
}
button {
  padding: 10px 20px;
  background-color: #28a745;
  border: none;
  color: white;
  border-radius: 4px;
  cursor: pointer;
}
button:hover {
  background-color: #218838;
}
.message {
  text-align: center;
  margin-top: 20px;
  font-size: 1.1rem;
```

```
      }
    </style>
  </head>
  <body>
    <h1>Create a New Post</h1>
    <form id="postForm">
      <label for="title">Post Title:</label>
      <input type="text" id="title"
name="title" required />

      <label for="body">Post Content:</label>
      <textarea id="body" name="body" rows="5"
required></textarea>

      <button type="submit">Submit
Post</button>
    </form>

    <div class="message"
id="formMessage"></div>

    <!-- Include the JavaScript file -->
    <script src="form.js"></script>
  </body>
</html>
```

Explanation:

- **Form Structure**:

  The form (`<form id="postForm">`) includes two fields—one for the post title and one for the post content—both marked as required.

- **Message Div**:

  The `<div id="formMessage">` will be used to display success or error messages based on the API response.

- **Styling**:

  Basic CSS is included for visual appeal and to make the form user-friendly.

Step 2: Capturing Form Data and Sending a POST Request

Create a file named **form.js** with the following code:

```
document.addEventListener('DOMContentLoaded',
() => {
  const postForm =
document.getElementById('postForm');
  const formMessage =
document.getElementById('formMessage');

  // Listen for form submission
  postForm.addEventListener('submit', (event)
=> {
    event.preventDefault();  // Prevent
default form submission behavior

    // Capture form data
```

```javascript
    const title =
document.getElementById('title').value.trim()
;
    const body =
document.getElementById('body').value.trim();

    // Clear any existing messages
    formMessage.textContent = '';

    // Validate form fields (basic
validation)
    if (!title || !body) {
      formMessage.textContent = 'Please fill
in both fields.';
      formMessage.style.color = 'red';
      return;
    }

    // Prepare data to send (as a JSON
object)
    const postData = {
      title: title,
      body: body,
      userId: 1  // Hard-coded user ID for
demonstration
    };

    // Send POST request to the test API
endpoint
```

```javascript
fetch('https://jsonplaceholder.typicode.com/p
osts', {
    method: 'POST',
    headers: {
      'Content-Type': 'application/json'
    },
    body: JSON.stringify(postData)
  })
    .then(response => {
      if (!response.ok) {
        throw new Error(`Server responded
with status: ${response.status}`);
      }
      return response.json();
    })
    .then(data => {
      // Display success message
      formMessage.textContent = `Post
created successfully with ID ${data.id}!`;
      formMessage.style.color = 'green';

      // Optionally, reset the form
      postForm.reset();
    })
    .catch(error => {
      // Display error message
      formMessage.textContent = `Error
submitting post: ${error.message}`;
      formMessage.style.color = 'red';
    });
```

```
  });
});
```

Explanation:

- **Event Listener:**
  DOMContentLoaded ensures the script runs after the HTML loads.
- **Prevent Default Behavior:**
  event.preventDefault() stops the form from submitting the default way and causing a page reload.
- **Data Capture and Validation:**
  The script retrieves values from the input fields, trims any extra white space, and performs basic validation.
- **POST Request:**
  A POST request is sent to
  https://jsonplaceholder.typicode.com/posts with the form data converted to JSON.
  - The request includes headers indicating the content type.
  - The response is checked for success before parsing.
- **Feedback:**
  Based on the outcome, a message is displayed in the #formMessage element. The text is styled in green for success and red for errors.

Exercises

1. **Additional Field**

o Modify the form to include a new input field for "Category". Update the JavaScript code to capture this new data and send it with the POST request.

2. **Input Validation Improvement**
   o Enhance validation to ensure the title is at least 5 characters long and the body is at least 10 characters long. Display a custom error message if these conditions are not met.

3. **Loading Indicator**
   o Before sending the POST request, display a "Submitting..." message. Once the request is complete, update the message to show success or error feedback.

4. **Clear Feedback After Delay**
   o Implement a mechanism that clears the success/error message after 5 seconds.

5. **Error Simulation**
   o Temporarily change the API endpoint URL to an incorrect one, observe the error message, then revert the change.

Multiple Choice Quiz

1. **What is the primary purpose of using `event.preventDefault()` in the form submission event handler?**

   A. To reset the form after submission.

   B. To prevent the default action of reloading the page upon form submission.

   C. To automatically validate the form fields.

   D. To allow the fetch request to run in the background.

2. **Which method is used to convert a JavaScript object into a JSON string before sending it in the POST request?**

   A. `JSON.parse()`

   B. `JSON.encode()`

   C. `JSON.stringify()`

   D. `JSON.toString()`

3. **Why is the header `Content-Type: 'application/json'` included in the POST request configuration?**

   A. It speeds up the request by compressing the data.

   B. It specifies to the server that the request body is in JSON format, so the server can parse it correctly.

   C. It allows the server to automatically convert the data into a JavaScript object.

   D. It is required by the browser for all HTTP requests.

4. **In the provided example, what happens if the API returns a non-successful HTTP status code?**

   A. The `.then()` block will still execute normally.

   B. The form is automatically resubmitted until a successful response is received.

   C. An error is thrown manually, which is then caught in the `.catch()` block.

   D. The fetch function will ignore the error and display a default message.

5. **Which property of the fetch response is used to check whether the response was successful before parsing it as JSON?**

   A. `response.data`

   B. `response.ok`

   C. `response.statusText`

   D. `response.body`

Detailed Answers to the Quiz

1. **(B) To prevent the default action of reloading the page upon form submission.**
   - ○ `event.preventDefault()` stops the browser from performing its default action (i.e., form submission and page reload), enabling you to handle the submission with JavaScript.

2. **(C) JSON.stringify()**
   - ○ This method converts a JavaScript object to a JSON string, which is required when sending the data in the body of a POST request.

3. **(B) It specifies to the server that the request body is in JSON format, so the server can parse it correctly.**
   - ○ The `Content-Type: application/json` header informs the server that the body of the request should be interpreted as JSON.

4. **(C) An error is thrown manually, which is then caught in the .catch() block.**
   - ○ If the API returns a non-successful HTTP status, the code checks `response.ok` and, if false, throws an error that is handled in the `.catch()` block.

5. **(B) response.ok**
   - ○ The `response.ok` property provides a Boolean indicating whether the HTTP status code is in the success range (200–299). It is used to determine if the response should be processed further or if an error should be thrown.

Conclusion

This section has demonstrated how to build a simple form that allows users to submit data to an API using the Fetch API with a POST request. You learned how to capture form data, perform basic validation, send it as JSON, and handle the server's response by providing clear user feedback. As you progress, you can extend these ideas to handle more complex forms, asynchronous operations, and better error handling, making your web applications both interactive and robust.

Asynchronous Syntax: Async/Await

Async/await is a modern way to handle asynchronous operations in JavaScript. It builds on top of promises but provides a cleaner, more readable syntax that is easier to write and understand, especially when dealing with multiple asynchronous steps.

Introduction to Async/Await

- **What is Async/Await?**
  Async/await is a syntactical feature in JavaScript that allows developers to write asynchronous code that looks and behaves more like synchronous code. It is built on promises.
- **Why is it Easier to Read and Write?**
  - **Sequential Flow:** Instead of chaining multiple `.then()` calls, async/await lets you write code in a top-down, sequential manner.
  - **Cleaner Error Handling:** Use traditional `try/catch` blocks, which are more intuitive than promise rejection handling with `.catch()`.

- ○ **Simpler Debugging**: The code flow is linear, making it easier to step through during debugging.

Rewriting Fetch Examples with Async/Await

Let's convert our earlier examples of GET and POST requests that used promises into async/await syntax.

Basic GET Request Using Async/Await

Example: Fetching a random dog image

```
// async-get-example.js
async function fetchRandomDog() {
  try {
    const response = await
fetch('https://dog.ceo/api/breeds/image/rando
m');

    // Check for HTTP errors
    if (!response.ok) {
      throw new Error(`HTTP error! status:
${response.status}`);
    }

    // Parse JSON data
    const data = await response.json();
    console.log('Random Dog Image URL:',
data.message);
  } catch (error) {
```

```
    // Handle network errors or manual thrown
errors
    console.error('Error fetching dog
image:', error.message);
  }
}


// Call the function
fetchRandomDog();
```

Explanation:

- **async function fetchRandomDog()**: Declares an asynchronous function.
- **await fetch(...)**: Waits for the promise returned by fetch to resolve.
- **Error Check**: If the response is not OK, we throw an error. This ensures that even HTTP errors (like 404 or 500) can be caught.
- **await response.json()**: Waits for the JSON parsing to complete.
- **try/catch Block**: Handles both network errors and errors thrown manually due to a non-OK response.

Basic POST Request Using Async/Await

Example: Submitting data to create a new post

```
// async-post-example.js
async function createPost() {
  const postData = {
    title: 'New Post with Async/Await',
```

```
    body: 'This post was created using
async/await syntax.',
    userId: 1,
  };

  try {
    const response = await
fetch('https://jsonplaceholder.typicode.com/p
osts', {
      method: 'POST',
      headers: { 'Content-Type':
'application/json' },
      body: JSON.stringify(postData),
    });

    // Check if response is successful
    if (!response.ok) {
      throw new Error(`Failed to create post.
Status: ${response.status}`);
    }

    const data = await response.json();
    console.log('Post Created:', data);
  } catch (error) {
    console.error('Error creating post:',
error.message);
  }
}

// Call the function
createPost();
```

Explanation:

- **`const postData`**: An object representing the data to be sent.
- **`await fetch(..., { method: 'POST', ... })`**: Sends a POST request.
- **Error Handling**: Uses `if (!response.ok)` to check for non-successful HTTP statuses, then throws an error.
- **`await response.json()`**: Parses the response once the fetch promise resolves.
- **`try/catch`**: Allows catching errors from both the network request and the parsing process.

Error Handling with Try/Catch

Using try/catch with async/await simplifies error handling:

- **Network Errors**: If `fetch` encounters a network error, the `await fetch()` call will reject and control will jump to the `catch` block.
- **API Errors**: After fetching, you can check the HTTP status using `response.ok` or `response.status`. If the response indicates a failure, throwing an error manually ensures it's handled in the `catch` block.
- **Synchronous Style**: Try/catch enables error handling similar to synchronous code, making the intent clearer.

Example with Detailed Error Handling:

```
// detailed-error-handling.js
async function getData(url) {
```

```javascript
  try {
    const response = await fetch(url);

    // Check for HTTP errors
    if (!response.ok) {
      if (response.status === 404) {
        throw new Error('Resource not found
(404).');
      } else if (response.status >= 500) {
        throw new Error('Server error. Please
try again later.');
      } else {
        throw new Error(`Unexpected error:
${response.status}`);
      }
    }

    const data = await response.json();
    return data;
  } catch (error) {
    // Log error and optionally rethrow or
return a default value
    console.error('Error fetching data:',
error.message);
    return null;
  }
}

// Usage example with async/await
async function displayData() {
```

```
  const data = await
getData('https://jsonplaceholder.typicode.com
/posts/1');
  if (data) {
    console.log('Post Data:', data);
  } else {
    console.log('Failed to fetch data.');
  }
}


// Call the function to display data
displayData();
```

Explanation:

- **Granular Error Messages**: The error handling differentiates between 404 (Not Found), 500+ (Server errors), and other HTTP errors.
- **Returning a Default Value**: In the case of an error, null is returned, which the caller can use to decide the next steps.

Exercises

1. **Async GET Request Modification**
    - Convert an existing promise-based GET request to async/await syntax.
    - Fetch a list of posts from https://jsonplaceholder.typicode.com/posts and log the title of the first post.

- Include error handling for both network errors and non-OK HTTP responses.

2. **Async POST Request Extension**
   - Create a function called `submitComment()` that uses async/await to send a POST request to `https://jsonplaceholder.typicode.com/comments`.
   - The function should send a JSON object with properties `postId`, `name`, `email`, and `body`.
   - Log the response data if successful, or log a custom error message if there is an error.

3. **Handling Multiple Async Calls**
   - Write an async function that first fetches user data from `https://jsonplaceholder.typicode.com/users` and then fetches posts for the first user using `https://jsonplaceholder.typicode.com/posts?userId={id}`.
   - Print both the user's name and their posts to the console.

4. **Error Handling Challenge**
   - Modify the above functions to simulate API errors (e.g., use an invalid URL) and observe how the try/catch block handles the errors.
   - Add custom messages depending on the type of error (e.g., "Resource not found", "Server error", etc.).

Multiple Choice Quiz

1. **What does the `async` keyword signify when used before a function in JavaScript?**

    A. It indicates that the function will run synchronously.

    B. It enables the function to use the `await` keyword, making it return a promise.

    C. It forces the function to execute in a separate thread.

    D. It marks the function for immediate execution.

2. **Which of the following is the correct way to wait for a promise to resolve using async/await?**

    A. `await promise.then()`.

    B. `var result = await promise;`.

    C. `promise.await()`.

    D. `await.then(promise)`.

3. **How can you handle errors in an async function?**

    A. By chaining multiple `.catch()` methods.

    B. Using a try/catch block around the awaited calls.

    C. Errors are handled automatically without any extra code.

    D. By using the `finally()` method alone.

4. **Which of the following best describes the advantage of async/await over traditional promise chaining?**

    A. It avoids the need for error handling.

    B. It makes asynchronous code look and behave more like synchronous code, improving readability and maintainability.

    C. It only works for GET requests.

    D. It eliminates the need for the Fetch API.

5. **In the async/await pattern, what will happen if a network error occurs during a fetch call?**

   A. The code execution will continue normally without interruption.

   B. The error will be caught in the associated try/catch block if one is present.

   C. The `await` statement automatically retries the fetch call.

   D. The promise returned by the async function will resolve with null.

Detailed Answers to the Quiz

1. **(B) It enables the function to use the `await` keyword, making it return a promise.**
   - Marking a function as `async` means you can use `await` inside it and the function will always return a promise, even if you return a non-promise value.

2. **(B) `var result = await promise;`.**
   - Using `await` in front of a promise will pause the execution of the async function until the promise resolves, assigning the resolved value to `result`.

3. **(B) Using a try/catch block around the awaited calls.**
   - Async/await supports error handling via try/catch, which captures any error thrown during the execution of awaited promises.

4. **(B) It makes asynchronous code look and behave more like synchronous code, improving readability and maintainability.**

- Async/await reduces the boilerplate and nested structure of multiple `.then()` calls, making the code easier to follow and debug.
5. **(B) The error will be caught in the associated try/catch block if one is present.**
   - If a network error causes the fetch promise to be rejected, the rejection is caught by the try/catch block surrounding the await statement.

Conclusion

Async/await simplifies asynchronous operations and makes handling asynchronous code much more intuitive. By converting traditional promise-based code into async/await format, you can write cleaner, more readable, and maintainable code. This section showed how to rewrite both GET and POST requests using async/await, and it provided strategies for effective error handling using try/catch blocks. As you continue, you'll find that using async/await improves both your productivity and the overall quality of your code when working with APIs.

Working with REST APIs

In this section, we will explore how to work effectively with REST APIs. You'll learn how to interpret API documentation, pass query parameters to refine your requests, understand basic authentication concepts with API keys or tokens, and deal with paginated responses. These concepts are crucial when working with real-world REST APIs, as they provide structure and standard practices for exchanging data between clients and servers.

API Documentation

Why API Documentation is Important:

- **Guidelines**: API documentation acts as a manual for developers, explaining available endpoints, request methods, required headers, query parameters, and the structure of responses.
- **Example Responses**: Documentation often provides sample requests and responses so you know what to expect.
- **Usage Limits**: Documentation typically includes information on rate limits, error codes, and best practices.

How to Read and Understand API Docs:

1. **Endpoints and Methods**:
   - Look for sections detailing the available endpoints (e.g., `/posts`, `/users/:id`) and their corresponding HTTP methods (GET, POST, etc.).
   - Check if the endpoint is for reading data (GET) or for modifying data (POST, PUT, DELETE).
2. **Parameters**:
   - **Path Parameters**: Part of the URL (e.g., `/users/{id}`); usually required.
   - **Query Parameters**: Appended to the URL after a question mark (e.g., `?filter=active&sort=desc`); used to refine the request.
3. **Headers**:
   - Required headers such as `Content-Type` and authentication tokens might be specified.
   - Some APIs require custom headers for specific functionality.
4. **Examples and Response Format**:

- Read through provided example requests and responses to understand the structure of returned JSON.
- Pay attention to HTTP status codes indicated in the documentation.

Query Parameters

Overview:

Query parameters allow you to pass additional information to an endpoint that can be used to filter, sort, or paginate data. They are added to the URL after a question mark (?) and separated by an ampersand (&).

Example: Filtering Data

Imagine you have an API endpoint that returns a list of posts. If you want to filter posts by category or search for a specific term, you might use query parameters:

```
const baseUrl =
'https://api.example.com/posts';
const queryParams =
'?category=technology&search=JavaScript';

// Complete URL becomes:
//
https://api.example.com/posts?category=techno
logy&search=JavaScript
```

```
fetch(baseUrl + queryParams)
  .then(response => response.json())
  .then(data => console.log('Filtered
Posts:', data))
  .catch(error => console.error('Error:',
error));
```

Tips:

- Always URL-encode parameter values using functions like `encodeURIComponent()` if they contain special characters.
- Refer to the API documentation to understand which query parameters are supported.

Authentication

Overview:

Many REST APIs require some level of authentication to ensure that only authorized users can access or modify resources. While authentication methods can vary in complexity, at the beginner level, you may encounter:

- **API Keys**: A unique identifier (often passed as a query parameter or header) that tells the server who you are.
- **Tokens**: A bearer token (usually provided after logging in) is sent with each request in a header, such as `Authorization: Bearer <token>`.

Example: Using an API Key in a Header

```
fetch('https://api.example.com/data', {
  headers: {
    'Authorization': 'Bearer
YOUR_API_TOKEN_HERE',
    'Content-Type': 'application/json'
  }
})
  .then(response => response.json())
  .then(data => console.log('Protected
Data:', data))
  .catch(error => console.error('Error:',
error));
```

Key Points:

- **Keep Keys Secure**: Never expose your API keys in client-side code in production environments. Use environment variables or server-side proxies to hide them.
- **Read Documentation**: APIs will outline how to include authentication—whether in headers, query parameters, or request bodies.

Paginated Data

What is Pagination?

Pagination is the process of dividing a large set of data into smaller chunks (pages). This is done to avoid sending massive amounts of data in a single response, which can be inefficient and slow.

How to Handle Paginated Responses:

1. **Identify Pagination Parameters**:

- o Common parameters include page, limit, offset, and per_page.
- o An API might return data along with metadata indicating the current page, total pages, or links to the next/previous pages.

2. **Example of a Paginated Request:**

```
const page = 1;
const limit = 10; // Number of items per page
const paginatedUrl =
`https://api.example.com/users?page=${page}&l
imit=${limit}`;

fetch(paginatedUrl)
   .then(response => response.json())
   .then(data => {
    // Process data.items (or whatever
property holds your items)
     console.log(`Users on Page ${page}:`,
data.items);
     // Optionally, look at data.total_pages
or data.next_page for navigation.
   })
   .catch(error => console.error('Error:',
error));
```

3. **Handling Pagination in Your Code:**
- o **Load More Button**: Allow users to click "Load More" to fetch the next page.
- o **Infinite Scroll**: Automatically load additional pages as the user scrolls.

- ○ **Navigation Controls**: Provide users with options to move to the next, previous, or a specific page.

Tips:

- Use the metadata provided by the API to understand how many pages exist and what the next page's URL should be.
- Consider performance and user experience when implementing pagination.

Exercises

1. **Reading Documentation Exercise**
   - ○ Find a public REST API (e.g., OpenWeatherMap, NewsAPI, or GitHub's API). Read its documentation and list:
     - Three endpoints along with their HTTP methods.
     - Two query parameters each endpoint accepts.
     - The authentication method required (if any).
   - ○ Write a short summary explaining how you would construct a GET request for one of the endpoints.
2. **Constructing Query Parameters**
   - ○ Write a function `buildUrl` that accepts a base URL and an object of query parameters and returns a URL with properly encoded query parameters. For example,
     `buildUrl('https://api.example.com/search', { q: 'JavaScript tutorials', page: 2 })` should return a properly formatted URL.

○ Test the function with different input objects.

3. **Implementing Authentication in Fetch**
    - ○ Write a sample fetch request that includes an API key in the header. Assume the API key is stored in a variable `apiKey`.
    - ○ Log the response data if the fetch is successful or output a meaningful error message if it fails.

4. **Handling Paginated Responses**
    - ○ Create a script that fetches the first two pages of user data from `https://jsonplaceholder.typicode.com/users` (simulate pagination by using query parameters like `?_page=1&_limit=5` and `?_page=2&_limit=5`).
    - ○ Merge and log the results from both pages, ensuring no duplicate entries.

Multiple Choice Quiz

1. **What is the primary purpose of API documentation?**
   A. To provide tutorials on front-end development.
   B. To explain the endpoints, methods, required parameters, and structure of API responses so developers know how to interact with the API.
   C. To automate all API requests without any extra code.
   D. To encrypt data before sending it to the server.

2. **How are query parameters added to an API request URL?**

A. By appending them to the URL after a hash symbol (#).

B. By inserting them directly into the URL path.

C. By appending them after a question mark (?), separated by ampersands (&) if there is more than one.

D. By adding them to the header of the HTTP request.

3. **Which header is commonly used to pass an API key or token for authentication?**

A. `Content-Length`

B. `Authorization`

C. `X-API-KEY`

D. `Accept-Language`

4. **What does a paginated API response typically include?**

A. The complete list of resources in one single response.

B. A subset of resources along with metadata such as the current page, total pages, and links to the next or previous pages.

C. Only the URL for the next page.

D. A random sample of all available resources.

5. **Which of the following best describes the use of `encodeURIComponent()` in constructing query parameters?**

A. It decodes encoded URLs so that they display as plain text.

B. It transforms special characters in query parameter values into a format that can be transmitted over the internet.

C. It encrypts the URL before making the fetch request.

D. It verifies the authenticity of the API key.

Detailed Answers to the Quiz

1. **(B) To explain the endpoints, methods, required parameters, and structure of API responses so developers know how to interact with the API.**
    - o API documentation is essential for understanding how to correctly use an API, including its endpoints, required parameters, and expected responses.
2. **(C) By appending them after a question mark (?), separated by ampersands (&) if there is more than one.**
    - o Query parameters are added to the URL using the ? symbol followed by key-value pairs, with multiple parameters separated by &.
3. **(B) Authorization**
    - o The Authorization header is commonly used to pass API keys or bearer tokens for authentication.
4. **(B) A subset of resources along with metadata such as the current page, total pages, and links to the next or previous pages.**
    - o Paginated responses help manage large data sets by returning a partial set of results along with useful metadata for navigating between pages.
5. **(B) It transforms special characters in query parameter values into a format that can be transmitted over the internet.**
    - o encodeURIComponent() ensures that characters not allowed in a URL (like spaces or symbols) are properly encoded.

Conclusion

Working with REST APIs involves more than just sending HTTP requests. You need to understand how to read API documentation, manage query parameters to filter and search data, implement basic authentication to securely access protected endpoints, and handle paginated responses to work with large data sets. With these skills, you'll be well-equipped to interact with a wide variety of REST APIs in your projects.

Debugging and Testing API Calls

When working with APIs, understanding how to debug and test your API calls is essential. Whether you're getting unexpected results, errors, or no response at all, effective debugging skills will help you diagnose and solve issues efficiently. In this section, we will explore how to use browser developer tools to inspect network requests, interpret request and response headers and payloads, and troubleshoot common issues like CORS errors and misconfigured headers or payloads.

Using Browser DevTools

Browser Developer Tools (DevTools) are indispensable for debugging API calls. Every major browser (Chrome, Firefox, Edge, Safari) includes a suite of tools that allow you to monitor, inspect, and test network activity.

Inspecting Network Requests

- **Network Tab Overview**:
    - Open your browser's DevTools (typically by pressing F12 or right-clicking and selecting "Inspect").

- o Navigate to the **Network** tab to view all HTTP requests made by the page.
- **What to Look For:**
  - o **Request URL:** Verify the correct endpoint is being called.
  - o **Request Method:** Confirm the HTTP method (GET, POST, etc.) is as intended.
  - o **Status Code:** Check whether the response status code is 2xx (successful) or indicates an error (e.g., 404, 500).
  - o **Response Payload:** Review the data returned from the server.
  - o **Headers:** Inspect both **Request Headers** (e.g., Content-Type, Authorization) and **Response Headers** (e.g., Content-Type, Cache-Control) to ensure they match expectations.

Understanding Request/Response Headers and Payloads

- **Request Headers:**
  - o Contain metadata such as `Content-Type` (telling the server the format of your data), authentication tokens, and custom headers.
- **Response Headers:**
  - o Include server responses, like the status code, data format, and cache settings.
- **Payloads:**
  - o The request payload is the body sent with a request (commonly seen with POST or PUT requests).
  - o The response payload is the data returned by the server, often in JSON format.

Example:
If your request is failing, use DevTools to click on the problematic request and carefully review the headers and payload in both the Request and Response sections. This information can be extremely helpful in identifying issues like incorrect endpoints, missing parameters, or misconfigured headers.

Debugging Common Errors

CORS Issues and How to Troubleshoot Them

CORS (Cross-Origin Resource Sharing) is a security feature implemented by browsers to restrict how web pages can make requests to a different domain than the one that served the web page. When CORS issues occur, you might see an error in the console like:

```
Access to fetch at
'https://api.example.com/data' from origin
'https://yourwebsite.com' has been blocked by
CORS policy: No 'Access-Control-Allow-Origin'
header is present on the requested resource.
```

Tips to Troubleshoot CORS Issues:

- **Understand the Error**: The error typically indicates that the server is not configured to accept requests from your domain.
- **Server-Side Fixes**:

- On the server, configure the response to include the `Access-Control-Allow-Origin` header with either a specific origin or the wildcard (*) if appropriate.
- **Local Testing Workarounds**:
  - Use a proxy server or CORS proxy for local development to bypass CORS restrictions.
  - For development only, some browsers or browser extensions allow you to disable CORS (not recommended for production).
- **Check Request Headers**: Ensure that you are not sending disallowed headers that might trigger a pre-flight OPTIONS request, which in turn might fail due to CORS policies.

Misconfigured Headers or Payloads

Errors can also arise from misconfigured headers or improperly formatted payloads. Common issues include:

- **Incorrect Content-Type**:
  - Ensure that the content type header matches the format of your request payload. For example, if you are sending JSON, the header should be `'Content-Type': 'application/json'`.
- **Malformed JSON**:
  - Use `JSON.stringify()` to convert JavaScript objects into valid JSON strings.
- **Missing Authentication Tokens**:
  - Verify that tokens or API keys are included in the request headers as required.

Example:
If your POST request returns a 400 Bad Request, double-check that:

- The JSON in your request body is correctly formatted.

- You have included all required headers.
- The API endpoint and URL are correct.

Coding Example: Debugging a Fetch Call

Below is an example that demonstrates how to catch and log errors, inspect the response, and provide meaningful error messages.

```
async function getUserData(userId) {
  const url =
`https://jsonplaceholder.typicode.com/users/$
{userId}`;

  try {
    const response = await fetch(url);

    // Debug: Log the response status and
headers
    console.log('Response Status:',
response.status);
    console.log('Response Headers:',
response.headers);

    if (!response.ok) {
      // Handle HTTP errors
      throw new Error(`HTTP error! status:
${response.status}`);
    }
```

```javascript
    const data = await response.json();
    console.log('User Data:', data);
    return data;
  } catch (error) {
    // This catch block handles network
errors or manually thrown errors
    console.error('Fetch Error:',
error.message);
    // Optionally, you can display the error
on the UI or log it to a remote server
    return null;
  }
}


// Call the function for testing
getUserData(1);
```

Explanation:

- The function getUserData fetches data for a given user ID.
- Before checking for HTTP errors, it logs the status and headers, which can be inspected in the browser console.
- If the response is not OK, it throws an error, and the catch block logs a meaningful error message.

Exercises

1. **Inspect a Network Request**

- Open your browser's DevTools, navigate to the Network tab, and perform a fetch request to `https://jsonplaceholder.typicode.com/posts`.
- Identify the Request URL, HTTP method, status code, and response headers.
- Write a short paragraph summarizing your observations.

2. **Simulate a CORS Issue**
   - Modify a fetch request to use an incorrect API endpoint (e.g., an endpoint on a different domain that doesn't allow cross-origin requests).
   - Observe and document the error message in the browser console.
   - Explain what steps you might take to address this issue on the server side.

3. **Test Misconfigured Headers**
   - Create a POST request that intentionally omits the `Content-Type` header and logs the error.
   - Modify the code to include the correct header, and observe the changes in behavior.
   - Write down your findings regarding how headers affect API responses.

4. **Debugging with Try/Catch**
   - Write a function that attempts to fetch a resource from an API endpoint.
   - Force an error by using an invalid URL and observe how the try/catch block handles it.
   - Output a custom error message to the console using `console.error()`.

5. **Analyze and Fix**

○ Provide a snippet of broken fetch code (simulate a common error such as malformed JSON or missing headers), and have students debug and correct it.

Multiple Choice Quiz

1. **Which tool in your web browser allows you to inspect network requests made by your JavaScript code?**
   A. Elements tab
   B. Console tab
   C. Network tab
   D. Sources tab

2. **What information can you NOT typically obtain from the Network tab in browser DevTools?**
   A. Request URL and HTTP method
   B. Response headers and status code
   C. The exact internal logic of the API server
   D. Response payload (data returned)

3. **How can you troubleshoot a CORS error?**
   A. Ensure that your JavaScript code is always minified.
   B. Verify that the server is configured to include an `Access-Control-Allow-Origin` header permitting your domain.
   C. Remove all headers from the request.
   D. Change the HTTP method from GET to POST.

4. **What might be the cause of a 400 Bad Request error when sending a POST request?**
   A. The API endpoint is correct but the request body is malformed.
   B. The server is down.
   C. The client has no internet connection.
   D. The response payload is empty.

5. **If you see an error message in your browser's console stating "Network Error", what does it imply?**

   A. The API returned a 200 OK status.

   B. The request could not reach the server, indicating a network-level issue.

   C. The server responded with a 500 Internal Server Error.

   D. The Fetch API automatically retries the request.

Detailed Answers to the Quiz

1. **(C) Network tab**
   - The Network tab in browser DevTools provides detailed information about all network requests including URLs, methods, headers, and responses.

2. **(C) The exact internal logic of the API server**
   - While the Network tab shows the request and response details, it does not show how the server processes the request internally.

3. **(B) Verify that the server is configured to include an `Access-Control-Allow-Origin` header permitting your domain.**
   - CORS errors are typically due to the server not allowing cross-origin requests. Configuring the server to include the appropriate `Access-Control-Allow-Origin` header is the solution.

4. **(A) The API endpoint is correct but the request body is malformed.**
   - A 400 Bad Request error commonly indicates that the payload was incorrect (e.g., misformatted JSON), resulting in the server not being able to process the request.

5. **(B) The request could not reach the server, indicating a network-level issue.**
   - "Network Error" generally implies that the browser was unable to complete the network request, often due to connectivity issues or unreachable servers.

Conclusion

Debugging and testing API calls is a critical skill for any developer working with the JavaScript Fetch API or REST APIs. Using browser DevTools to inspect requests, review headers and payloads, and diagnose common errors—such as CORS issues or misconfigured request headers—can save you time and frustration. With the techniques covered in this section, you'll be better equipped to identify, troubleshoot, and fix issues in your API calls, leading to more robust and reliable applications.

Building a Mini Project

In this section, you'll build a mini project that consolidates all you've learned about the Fetch API, REST APIs, error handling, async/await, and debugging. The project we'll develop is a **User Directory**—an application that fetches user data from an API, displays it in an organized manner, and handles user interactions with search and filtering features.

Project Idea: User Directory

Overview:

Build a web application that displays a list of users. Users can view details such as name, username, email, and address. You can also add features such as filtering/searching for a user. This project simulates real-world applications where the frontend needs to interact with a remote API to retrieve and display data.

Data Source:

For demonstration purposes, we'll use the public API JSONPlaceholder, which returns an array of user objects in JSON format.

Key Concepts in Action

1. **Fetching Data:**
   - Use the Fetch API to retrieve a list of users.
   - Handle asynchronous operations with either Promises or async/await.
2. **Displaying Data:**
   - Dynamically update the HTML DOM to show user data.
   - Create templates or components (e.g., user cards or list items) to display details.
3. **User Interactions:**
   - Add interactive elements such as a search box.
   - Allow users to filter the directory by name or username.
   - Provide feedback messages (e.g., "No users found").
4. **Error Handling and Loading States:**
   - Show a loading indicator while fetching data.
   - Display error messages when the API call fails.

○ Use try/catch (or promise `.catch()`) to gracefully handle errors.

Enhancements for a Polished Experience

1. **Loading Indicators:**
   - ○ Display a spinner or "Loading..." message until the data is fully loaded.
   - ○ Remove the indicator once the data is displayed.
2. **Error Messages:**
   - ○ Provide clear error messages if the API call fails or if filtering returns no results.
   - ○ Optionally, allow users to retry the fetch operation.
3. **Responsive Design:**
   - ○ Use basic CSS or frameworks like Bootstrap to ensure the directory displays well on mobile and desktop.
   - ○ Enhance the visual appeal with hover effects and card layouts.
4. **Advanced Features (Optional):**
   - ○ Implement pagination if the dataset is large.
   - ○ Offer a "details" view when a user card is clicked.
   - ○ Integrate a modal pop-up for additional user information.

Coding Example: User Directory

Below is a simplified implementation of a User Directory using HTML, CSS, and JavaScript with async/await for fetching data, basic filtering, loading feedback, and error handling.

HTML (index.html)

```html
<!DOCTYPE html>
<html lang="en">
<head>
  <meta charset="UTF-8">
  <title>User Directory</title>
  <style>
    body { font-family: Arial, sans-serif;
margin: 20px; }
    .container { max-width: 800px; margin:
auto; }
    h1 { text-align: center; }
    #loading { text-align: center; font-size:
1.2rem; }
    #error { color: red; text-align: center;
}
    #searchBox { width: 100%; padding: 10px;
margin-bottom: 20px; }
    .user-card {
      border: 1px solid #ccc;
      border-radius: 5px;
      padding: 15px;
      margin-bottom: 10px;
      box-shadow: 1px 1px 5px
rgba(0,0,0,0.1);
    }
  </style>
</head>
<body>
  <div class="container">
    <h1>User Directory</h1>
```

```html
    <input type="text" id="searchBox"
placeholder="Search by name or username..."
/>
    <div id="loading">Loading users...</div>
    <div id="error"></div>
    <div id="userDirectory"></div>
  </div>
  <script src="app.js"></script>
</body>
</html>
```

JavaScript (app.js)

```javascript
// Wait for the DOM to fully load
document.addEventListener('DOMContentLoaded',
initApp);

async function initApp() {
  const loadingEl =
document.getElementById('loading');
  const errorEl =
document.getElementById('error');
  const userDirectoryEl =
document.getElementById('userDirectory');
  const searchBox =
document.getElementById('searchBox');

  try {
    // Fetch users from JSONPlaceholder
    const users = await fetchUsers();
    // Remove the loading indicator
```

```javascript
      loadingEl.style.display = 'none';
      // Display all users initially
      displayUsers(users, userDirectoryEl);

      // Add event listener for search
filtering
      searchBox.addEventListener('input', (e)
=> {
         const query =
e.target.value.toLowerCase();
         const filteredUsers = users.filter(user
=>

user.name.toLowerCase().includes(query) ||

user.username.toLowerCase().includes(query)
         );
         // Clear previous results and display
new filtered users
         userDirectoryEl.innerHTML = '';
         if (filteredUsers.length > 0) {
            displayUsers(filteredUsers,
userDirectoryEl);
         } else {
            userDirectoryEl.innerHTML = '<p>No
users found.</p>';
         }
      });
   } catch (error) {
      loadingEl.style.display = 'none';
```

```javascript
    errorEl.textContent = `Error:
${error.message}`;
  }
}

// Function to fetch users using async/await
async function fetchUsers() {
  const response = await
fetch('https://jsonplaceholder.typicode.com/u
sers');
  if (!response.ok) {
    throw new Error(`Failed to fetch users:
${response.status}`);
  }
  return response.json();
}

// Function to display a list of users
function displayUsers(users, container) {
  users.forEach(user => {
    const card =
document.createElement('div');
    card.className = 'user-card';
    card.innerHTML = `
      <h2>${user.name}
(${user.username})</h2>
      <p><strong>Email:</strong>
${user.email}</p>
```

```
        <p><strong>Address:</strong>
${user.address.suite},
${user.address.street},
${user.address.city}</p>
    `;
    container.appendChild(card);
  });
}
```

Explanation:

- **HTML:**
  - The page includes an input field for searching, a loading message that is visible until data is loaded, an error message area, and a container to display user cards.
- **JavaScript:**
  - The `initApp()` function is the main entry point. It uses `fetchUsers()` to retrieve data, then calls `displayUsers()` to show the user cards on the page.
  - A search box filters users in real time by listening for input changes.
  - Error handling is integrated using try/catch, so if fetching fails, a user-friendly error is displayed.
  - Loading indicators are managed by showing/hiding elements based on the state of the fetch operation.

Exercises

1. **Enhance the Directory:**

- Extend the project to include a "View Details" button on each user card. When clicked, display additional details (e.g., company name, phone number) in a modal or separate section.
- **Hint:** You can capture the user's data on button click and then dynamically create the modal content.

2. **Implement Pagination:**
    - Simulate pagination by only displaying 5 users per page and adding buttons to navigate between pages.
    - **Hint:** Use a combination of slicing the users array and updating the displayed cards on click events.

3. **Custom Loading Indicator:**
    - Replace the simple "Loading users..." text with a more sophisticated loading spinner or animation.
    - **Hint:** You might use a CSS animation or an animated GIF.

4. **Error Simulation:**
    - Temporarily modify the fetch URL (e.g., add an extra character) to simulate an error. Observe the error handling in action and then revert the change.
    - **Hint:** Observe the error message displayed in the `#error` element.

5. **Advanced Search Filters:**
    - Add additional filters (e.g., by city) to the search functionality.
    - **Hint:** Expand the filter function in the search event listener to include more properties from the user objects.

Multiple Choice Quiz

1. **What is the primary goal of the mini project described in this section?**

   A. To build a complete back-end server.

   B. To create a User Directory that fetches, displays, and allows filtering of user data from an API.

   C. To learn how to use CSS frameworks like Bootstrap.

   D. To implement complex server authentication.

2. **Which API endpoint is used in the project to fetch user data?**

   A.
   `https://jsonplaceholder.typicode.com/posts`

   B.
   `https://jsonplaceholder.typicode.com/users`

   C. `https://api.example.com/users`

   D.
   `https://api.openweathermap.org/data/2.5/users`

3. **How does the project provide feedback to the user during data fetching?**

   A. By reloading the page continuously.

   B. Using a loading indicator (e.g., "Loading users...") that is hidden once data is loaded.

   C. By redirecting to a different URL.

   D. Through multiple alert pop-ups.

4. **What happens if no user matches the search query in the project?**

   A. The search box clears automatically.

   B. The entire application crashes.

   C. A message "No users found." is displayed.

   D. The API is called again automatically.

5. **Which of the following is NOT an enhancement suggested for the project?**

   A. Adding loading indicators.

   B. Displaying error messages.

   C. Integrating a user login system with OAuth.

   D. Implementing pagination.

Detailed Answers to the Quiz

1. **(B) To create a User Directory that fetches, displays, and allows filtering of user data from an API.**
   - The project is designed to showcase basic API consumption, dynamic data display, and user interaction with filtering features.

2. **(B)**
   `https://jsonplaceholder.typicode.com/use rs`
   - The project fetches user data from JSONPlaceholder's /`users` endpoint.

3. **(B) Using a loading indicator (e.g., "Loading users...") that is hidden once data is loaded.**
   - A loading message is shown until the data is fetched and rendered.

4. **(C) A message "No users found." is displayed.**
   - When the search filter returns no matching results, the interface displays a clear message indicating the absence of results.

5. **(C) Integrating a user login system with OAuth.**
   - While user authentication can be an advanced feature, it is not part of the suggested enhancements for this beginner-level mini project.

Conclusion

Building a mini project like a User Directory is a great way to apply the concepts you've learned about the Fetch API and working with REST APIs. Through this project, you've practiced fetching data, dynamically rendering it on a webpage, handling user interactions, and enhancing the user experience with loading indicators and error messages. As you continue to develop your skills, consider adding more advanced features and improvements to further refine your project and prepare for real-world applications.

Next Steps and Best Practices

After mastering the basics of JavaScript's Fetch API and REST APIs, it's time to explore some advanced topics and best practices. This section introduces an alternative to Fetch (Axios), touches on important concepts like rate limiting and caching, and describes best practices for writing secure, maintainable, and robust API integration code.

Advanced Topics

Axios (as an alternative to Fetch)

Axios is a popular JavaScript library that provides an easier interface for making HTTP requests. Some advantages include:

- **Simplified Syntax**: Axios automatically parses JSON responses and has built-in support for request timeouts.

- **Interceptors**: These allow you to intercept requests or responses to add logic (such as logging, error handling, or adding authentication headers).
- **Browser and Node.js Support**: Axios works seamlessly both on the client and the server.

Example: A simple GET request using Axios

```
// Install Axios via npm: npm install axios
// Or include via a CDN in your HTML file.

axios.get('https://jsonplaceholder.typicode.com/users')
  .then(response => {
    console.log('Users:', response.data);
  })
  .catch(error => {
    console.error('Error fetching users:',
error);
  });
```

Comparison with Fetch:

- **Error Handling**: Axios treats HTTP error status codes (like 404 or 500) as errors automatically, whereas with Fetch you need to check response.ok.
- **Response Data**: Axios automatically transforms JSON data, eliminating the extra step of calling .json().

API Rate Limiting and Caching

- **API Rate Limiting:**

- Many APIs enforce a limit on the number of requests you can make in a given period (e.g., 1000 requests per hour).
- **Why It Matters:** Exceeding these limits can lead to denied or throttled requests.
- **Strategies:**
    - Implement request throttling in your application.
    - Cache responses to reduce the number of API calls.
    - Monitor the API's response headers; many APIs include remaining request quota information.

- **Caching:**
    - Caching involves storing a copy of a response so that subsequent requests can be served faster.
    - **Techniques:**
        - **Browser caching:** Utilize HTTP cache headers (`Cache-Control`, `ETag`).
        - **Client-side caching:** Store responses in local storage or in-memory objects.
        - **Service Workers:** In progressive web apps (PWAs), service workers can intercept network requests and return cached responses.

Best Practices

Modularizing Fetch Logic

- **Why Modularize?**

- By isolating your API calls into separate modules or functions, you improve code reusability and maintainability.

Example Structure:

```
// api.js
export async function getUsers() {
  const response = await
fetch('https://jsonplaceholder.typicode.com/u
sers');
  if (!response.ok) {
    throw new Error(`Error:
${response.status}`);
  }
  return response.json();
}
```

-
- Then import and use these functions in your application logic.

Securing API Keys

- **Do Not Expose Keys:**
  - Avoid hardcoding API keys in your JavaScript code that runs on the client side.
- **Environment Variables:**
  - When using build tools or server environments, store API keys in environment variables.
- **Server-Side Proxy:**

- Route API calls through your server so that keys remain secret. The server can then inject authentication headers before passing the request to the external API.

Validating and Sanitizing Data

- **Input Validation:**
  - Always validate data received from an API. Check that the data conforms to the expected structure and type before processing.
- **Data Sanitization:**
  - Sanitize any user input or API-provided data especially before inserting it into the DOM to prevent XSS (Cross-Site Scripting) attacks.

Example:

```
function sanitizeHTML(str) {
  const tempDiv =
document.createElement('div');
  tempDiv.textContent = str;
  return tempDiv.innerHTML;
}

// Usage when displaying data:
const userName = sanitizeHTML(user.name);
element.innerHTML = `<p>${userName}</p>`;
```

- **Schema Validation:**
  - Use libraries like Joi or Yup to validate JSON structures.

Exercises

1. **Axios Experiment:**
   - Replace a basic Fetch GET request in one of your projects with an Axios GET request.
   - Compare the code and note the differences in error handling.
   - Write a brief summary of your experience and any challenges you encountered.

2. **Rate Limiting Simulation:**
   - Simulate API rate limiting by writing a function that limits the number of API calls to a maximum of 5 per minute.
   - Use JavaScript's `setTimeout` or a throttling library (like lodash's `throttle`) to control the request rate.
   - Log each request attempt with a timestamp to observe the throttling in action.

3. **Modularizing Fetch:**
   - Create a module (e.g., `api.js`) that exports functions for fetching users, posts, and comments from JSONPlaceholder.
   - Import these functions into another file and build a simple interface that displays the fetched data.
   - Ensure your module includes error handling and input validation.

4. **Securing API Keys (Conceptual):**
   - Research how to use environment variables in your preferred build tool or server framework (e.g., Webpack, Node.js).
   - Write a short guide on how you would prevent exposing API keys in a production build.

5. **Data Validation and Sanitization:**

- o Build a form that collects data (e.g., a comment submission form).
- o Write JavaScript code that validates the input to ensure it is not empty and sanitizes it before display.
- o Show a warning message if the input fails validation.

Multiple Choice Quiz

1. **What is one advantage of using Axios over the Fetch API?**
   A. Axios requires no error handling.
   B. Axios automatically transforms JSON responses and treats non-2xx responses as errors.
   C. Axios is built into modern browsers.
   D. Axios can only be used on the server side.

2. **Why is API rate limiting important for developers to consider?**
   A. It improves the user interface.
   B. It prevents developers from overloading the API with too many requests, which can lead to throttled or blocked requests.
   C. It guarantees that an API call will always succeed.
   D. It encrypts the data before transmission.

3. **Which of the following is a best practice when working with API keys on the client side?**
   A. Hardcode the API key directly into your JavaScript files.
   B. Store the API key in an environment variable or use a server-side proxy to keep it secure.
   C. Append the API key to every URL as a query parameter.
   D. Print the API key in the browser console for debugging purposes.

4. **How can you improve the maintainability of your API calls in your codebase?**

   A. Write all API calls in-line with your DOM manipulation code.

   B. Modularize your fetch logic by separating API calls into independent functions or modules.

   C. Avoid using any error handling to reduce code complexity.

   D. Always use synchronous calls to ensure consistency.

5. **What is a common method for sanitizing user input before inserting it into the DOM?**

   A. Using JSON.stringify()

   B. Utilizing innerHTML without modifications

   C. Creating a temporary DOM element and setting its textContent to the user input, then retrieving the sanitized value from innerHTML

   D. Directly inserting user input as-is since browsers sanitize it automatically

---

Detailed Answers to the Quiz

1. **(B) Axios automatically transforms JSON responses and treats non-2xx responses as errors.**
   - Axios provides a simpler and more robust API by handling JSON transformations and error responses out-of-the-box.

2. **(B) It prevents developers from overloading the API with too many requests, which can lead to throttled or blocked requests.**
   - API rate limiting ensures that services remain available and perform well for all users by controlling the number of allowed requests.

3. **(B) Store the API key in an environment variable or use a server-side proxy to keep it secure.**
   - Exposing API keys in client-side code can lead to security vulnerabilities. Best practices involve keeping keys hidden from the user.
4. **(B) Modularize your fetch logic by separating API calls into independent functions or modules.**
   - Modularizing the code improves readability, maintainability, and reusability across different parts of your application.
5. **(C) Creating a temporary DOM element and setting its textContent to the user input, then retrieving the sanitized value from innerHTML**
   - This method ensures that any potentially harmful code in the user input is rendered as plain text rather than executable HTML.

In this final section, we explored advanced topics and best practices to further enhance your API integration skills. Beyond using the Fetch API, alternatives like Axios can simplify many tasks, while concepts like rate limiting and caching are crucial for performance and scalability. Following best practices—such as modularizing your code, securing API keys, and validating/sanitizing data—will help ensure that your code is robust, secure, and maintainable. As you continue developing more complex applications, these advanced techniques and best practices will prove invaluable in building professional-grade web applications.

By understanding these topics and implementing the provided exercises, you'll be well on your way to mastering API integrations in JavaScript and preparing for real-world application development.

Conclusion

As you complete **"JavaScript Fetch API for Complete Beginners"**, you've taken a significant step toward mastering one of the most essential skills in modern web development. Understanding how to effectively work with APIs and the Fetch API opens the door to creating dynamic, interactive, and data-driven applications.

The skills and knowledge you've gained throughout this book are not just theoretical; they are practical tools you can apply to real-world projects. Whether you're building your first web app or refining your professional development skills, the concepts and exercises in this book serve as a foundation for deeper exploration.

Remember, becoming proficient in web development is a journey of continuous learning and experimentation. As you encounter new challenges, return to the principles and techniques you've learned here, and don't hesitate to expand your knowledge by diving into more advanced topics.

Thank you for choosing this book as part of your learning journey. Keep coding, keep creating, and, most importantly, keep challenging yourself to reach new heights. The world of JavaScript and web development is vast—explore it boldly and confidently.

About the Author

Laurence Lars Svekis is a distinguished web developer, sought-after educator, and best-selling author, renowned for his profound contributions to JavaScript development and modern web programming education. With over two decades of experience in web application development, Laurence has become a leading authority in the field, empowering developers worldwide with his clear, insightful, and practical approach to complex coding concepts.

Laurence specializes in JavaScript, functional programming, asynchronous programming, and front-end web development. His deep technical expertise, combined with a passion for teaching, allows him to deliver comprehensive courses and resources that simplify even the most challenging programming topics. Through his content, Laurence equips learners with practical skills to build scalable, maintainable, and efficient applications.

With over one million students worldwide, Laurence's interactive courses, books, and live presentations have become a cornerstone for developers looking to master JavaScript. His hands-on teaching style, enriched with real-world examples, coding exercises, and projects, makes advanced topics like closures, promises, and async programming accessible to learners of all levels.

In addition to being a prolific author, Laurence actively contributes to the broader web development community by sharing insights, fostering collaboration, and mentoring developers. His ability to break down complex technical concepts into simple, actionable steps has earned him a reputation as a trusted and inspiring voice in JavaScript education.

www.ingramcontent.com/pod-product-compliance
Lightning Source LLC
LaVergne TN
LVHW051248050326
832903LV00028B/2637